DEVELOPMENT: A CHAL

STUDIES IN THE SOCIAL SCIENCES

edited by C. A. O. van Nieuwenhuijze

10

DEVELOPMENT
A CHALLENGE TO WHOM?

AN ESSAY ON THE PRESENT STATE AND THE NEXT STAGE
IN DEVELOPMENT STUDIES,
WITH SPECIAL REFERENCE TO SOCIOLOGY
AND WITH EXAMPLES FROM THE MIDDLE EAST

by

C. A. O. VAN NIEUWENHUIJZE

Institute of Social Studies, The Hague

1969

MOUTON

THE HAGUE • PARIS

HD
82
N 53

Printed in The Netherlands by Mouton & Co., Printers, The Hague.

Let it be a challenge to you.
(Bel Kaufman, *Up the Down Staircase*.)

L'important en effet n'est pas d'essayer de regarder l'avenir, mais d'y apporter un certain état d'esprit.
(Bernard Cazes, in *History and Theory* VI/3.)

During a Bureau of Indian Affairs (BIA) conference, an Alaskan Indian rose and spoke: "I've been reading Kierkegaard." (You could hear a pin drop.) "He says there are these three basic fears that confront a man – marriage, God and death. I want to add a fourth fear – change."
(*The Christian Science Monitor*, June 5, 1968, p. 1.)

FOREWORD

This essay is the product of a coincidence. The Institute of Social Studies at The Hague, the Netherlands, which I have served since its beginning, celebrated its fifteenth anniversary. This is not a respectable age, but it does offer occasion for reflection. Fifteen years ago there was no such thing as development studies and we had to start from scratch. Having worked for so many years on a trial and error basis to a large extent, one wants to know where one stands.

At the same time, I was invited to visit a number of emerging centres of studies on development and related subjects, sometimes for consultation, sometimes for lectures or seminars. This again provided good cause for thought, mostly on questions like where do we go from here.

Thus prompted on two sides, I found myself trying to sum up what is the present state of development studies and also what are the issues, emerging now, that we are likely to face in the coming years. In trying to express some ideas on the matter, I have naturally concentrated on the discipline of my predilection, sociology, and on the area on which my ignorance is rather less than on other areas, the Middle East. Even so, I have sought for occasions to overstep the boundaries that thus seemed to impose themselves, in the conviction that what we need most nowadays is a general conspectus.

This is the occasion to give thanks for opportunities for discussion, offered by Professor James J. Heaphy, Director, Comparative Studies Program, Graduate School of Public Affairs, State University of New York at Albany; Professor Howard A. Reed, Director, Institute of International and Intercultural Studies, College of Liberal Arts and Sciences, University of Connecticut, Storrs; Professor William K. Medlin, Study Group on Education and Nation Building, School of Education, University of Michigan, Ann Arbor; Professor Egbert de Vries, Graduate School of Public and International Affairs, University of Pittsburgh; Professor Paul O. Proehl, Director, African Studies Center, University of California at Los Angeles; Professor Gustave E. von Grunebaum, Director, Near Eastern Center, University of California at Los Angeles, who in addition was kind enough to read an earlier draft of this essay and give his helpful comments; Dr. Everett R. Clinchy, The Institute on Man and Science, New York, N.Y. Mr. H. G. Quik, Director of the Netherlands Universities' Foundation for International Co-operation at The Hague, proved a most challenging critic during the process of writing and has stimulated the effort in a manner for which I am very grateful. Dr. G. van den Steenhoven, of Nijmegen Catholic University, read the first draft and gave helpful comments. Professor J. van Baal, Utrecht University, read the entire final draft and provided a number of corrections and penetrating observations of which I have tried to make the best use. Like thanks, for both critique and encouragement, are due to Professor L. H. Janssen S.J., Catholic School of Economics, Tilburg.

In these thanks I wish to include numerous friends in all countries of the Middle East, with whom I have in the course of the years had occasion to discuss problems like the ones that are to come up in this essay. Knowing the nature and frequency of my movements throughout the area, they will understand and forgive that I refrain from an attempt to list names of persons or institutions. The many and regular contacts that I have enjoyed as Secretary General, and later as a member of the Steering Committee, of the Mediterranean Social Sciences Research Council, have been a constant source of inspiration. A series of visits to Iran, for purposes of consultation at Pahlavi University, Shiraz, has in its turn proved invaluable as a source of ideas.

The manuscript of this work resulted from the dedicated effort, here gratefully acknowledged, of Miss R. W. Baas.

The Hague, Summer 1968.

The title of this essay recalls an older publication entitled *The Challenge of Development*, Jerusalem (Hebrew Univ., Eliezer Kaplan School), 1958. There exists at least one more book under the same title, namely by Richard J. Ward (ed.) (Chicago, Aldine, 1967).

CONTENTS

VI. DEVELOPMENT: A CHALLENGE TO WHOM?

PART I

INTRODUCTION

1

DEVELOPMENT A NORMAL CONCERN

The present generation in virtually all countries of the world are ac-customed to consider development as a major concern: if not directly to themselves at least to their political and economic leaders.

As one signal problem of an entire period of world history (or should one say, of the initial period of "one-world" history?), development has been with us for the last twenty years or so. It emerged gradually, in the aftermath of World War II. Speaking in terms of American history, one may perhaps say that it emerged during the interval between Roose-velt's Four Freedoms and Truman's Point Four. Indeed, it is Truman's Inaugural Address, January 4th, 1949, that inscribes development in the agenda of urgent world business,

Fourth, we must embark on a bold new program for making the benefits of our scientific advances and industrial progress available for the improve-ment and growth of underdeveloped areas.

More than half of the people of the world are living in conditions ap-proaching misery. Their food is inadequate. They are victims of disease. Their economic life is primitive and stagnant. Their poverty is a handicap and a threat both to them and to more prosperous areas.

For the first time in history, humanity possesses the knowledge and the skill to relieve the suffering of these people.

The United States is pre-eminent among nations in the development of industrial and scientific techniques. The material resources which we can afford to use for the assistance of other peoples are limited. But our imponderable resources in technical knowledge are constantly growing and are inexhaustible.

I believe that we should make available to peace-loving peoples the benefits of our store of technical knowledge in order to help them realize their aspirations for a better life. And, in co-operation with other nations, we should foster capital investment in areas needing development.

Our aim should be to help the free peoples of the world, through their own efforts, to produce more food, more clothing, more materials for housing, and more mechanical power to lighten their burdens.

We invite other countries to pool technological resources in this undertaking. Their contributions will be warmly welcomed. This should be a co-operative enterprise in which all nations work together through the United Nations and its specialized agencies wherever practicable. It must be a world-wide effort for the achievement of peace, plenty, and freedom.

In re-reading this statement, one has occasion to wonder whether it still stands. Suppose that we were now preparing the celebration of the twentieth anniversary of Point Four: would it make sense to solemnly re-read the statement, or would it have to be updated, and, to the purpose, more or less fundamentally revised? There could appear to be grounds for the solemn repeating of Truman's phrases. Indeed there is much in the practice of international assistance, and also in the general manner in which development is conceived and discussed, that gives the impression of firm continuity. Surely, in these twenty years a number of trodden paths have come into use, and a number of paradigms have become established, that many would be quite hesitant to relinquish. But surely, one realizes – not without some shock – that any and every instance of trodden paths and established paradigms in this connection is necessarily something like a contradiction in terms. It would seem to signal non-development in matters of development, stagnation where everything should be a-move. The question is thus bound to arise whether this outward appearance of things does afford a true picture of the real state of affairs in matters of development.

Changing ideas about development

It is my intention, on this occasion, to argue that the answer to this question must be in the negative. More precisely, I intend to draw attention to the fact, as yet insufficiently recognized and accounted for, that during the practice of about twenty years' concern with development, a number of the initial considerations have changed. So much so that development action has had to change, sometimes imperceptibly sometimes visibly, and that it is bound to change even more and perhaps also more noticeably.

This shift in the state of affairs is partly a matter of correction applied to incorrect premises. For another part, it is a matter of changing conditions. These in their turn represent a fairly complicated proposition. For one thing, one would hope that changing conditions would be, mainly or entirely, in consequence of purposeful development action. For another matter, one realizes that numerous "historical forces", far from concerted, are at work simultaneously. If this were not enough, one realizes furthermore that development action does hardly ever occur in pure form: being mixed up, most of the time at most places, with action that is quite differently motivated and directed.

For the sake of clear arguing, it should be nice if we could enumerate and discuss, first, shifts in ideas about development and in development action that could be ascribed to correction in premisses, and subsequently shifts due to changes in conditions, these in their turn to be differentiated according to type, and enumerated accordingly. Unfortunately no such organization of the argument appears possible. The various aspects or motive forces that one would like to distinguish for systematic purposes are mixed or blurred in the large majority of cases.

Neither would it seem fair to take President Truman's statement and use it item by item as so many pegs on which to hang an argument. It was not intended for such use.

In presenting my thoughts I shall thus have to resort to less systematic devices, simply discussing a number of aspects in some order that seems convenient.

2

DEVELOPED VERSUS UNDERDEVELOPED

There is at least one issue that is clearly and predominantly a matter of correction of premisses.

It refers to the conception that people have of development. As is perhaps inevitable with a concept like this, the matter is uncomfortably broad and ramified. I will venture to indicate a few signal points.

It appears that we are gradually moving away from one conception of development and thus find ourselves in increasingly urgent need to replace it by another, more viable one. The conception with which we get more and more disenchanted represents a curious combination of ethnocentrism on the one hand and progressivism on the other, – the latter in its turn being an odd mixture of deterministic and mechanistic conceptions.

The disminishing returns of ethnocentrism

Ethnocentrism is the normal corollary of the existence of sociocultural entities, such as empires, cultures, nations, also tribes or extended families. Its relatively unchecked manifestation, which we are inclined to consider perfectly normal, is in fact typical for conditions of what may be called – with a name paralleling a term of economics – imperfect coordination: namely of sociocultural entities in a world-wide context. Considered from a "one world" viewpoint, unbridled ethnocentrism is little more than a case of cultural lag. But that is another matter. What ethnocentrism means today, and what it has meant for millennia, is that the member of a given sociocultural entity conceives of the universe as somehow an extension of this particular entity, which for all practical and theoretical purposes is his world. Consequently, he will account for the occurrence of any sociocultural entities not his own in such a manner as to vindicate the unique, that is universal, character of his own. Almost everyone is aware of examples of how those belonging to a given "we" are called "humans" or "civilized" and those not belonging are called, by contradistinction, non-human or subhuman or uncivilized. Barbarian means jabberer. Surely, if in this kind of accounting process the concept of development happens to feature as a signal notion, what will inevitably happen is that the "we" involved will feature as developed and the non-we, the "they" involved accordingly as non-developed. Non-developed may sometimes be rendered categorically as undeveloped; sometimes it may appear more relativistically as underdeveloped.

The curious euphemism thanks to which undeveloped may at times appear as underdeveloped relates to the other characteristic mentioned: progressivism. Un-developed, if envisaged in a historical perspective of evolutionism of a more or less deterministic, more or less mechanistic nature, is bound to appear as a relative not an absolute phenomenon. This is what the term underdeveloped is meant to convey. The older usage of the term primitives, as distinct from barbarians, connotes much the same thing. The "we" that is central to the (= our) universe, accounts for the "they" that is a complication to this universe in the manner of a modified rejection. Short of passing a verdict that "they" are not human, it is postulated that "they" are not quite human, or, with the historical perspective added, not yet fully human. In other words, "they" are relegated to the far end of a historical sequence that is envisaged in a thoroughly evolutionistic manner: a more or less straight line leading from scratch to perfection.[1] The manner in which this quasi-historical perspective is employed in dealing with contemporaries is neither particularly elegant nor particularly sophisticated. In fact, it is fiendishly simple. The underdeveloped peoples of today are simply assumed to be where "our" forebears were ages ago. Consequently, their primary need is to catch up with us. Moreover, we are the ones who are in a position to tell them how to do this. Surprisingly enough, this view of things seems not at all difficult to corroborate. Material wealth, technological "advancement", and the like prove fully serviceable as apparently irrefutable cases in point.

Underdevelopment: term of doubtful significance

Even so, the inspiration of the romantic age conspires with certain harsh experiences of development action to breed some uneasiness and at times even second thoughts on the matter. In quite a few cases, those immediately concerned do not muster the brutal courage that would be

---

[1] Cultural evolutionism as reflected in attitudes towards development and biological evolutionism as apparent in racism and the like are in exactly the same position in this regard. Comp. C. Lévi-Strauss, "Race and History", in *The Race Question in Modern Science* (Paris-New York [UNESCO], 1956), esp. p. 125 ff.

needed to declare a given sociocultural entity completely underdeveloped. Most people will feel somewhat uneasy if asked to pass a verdict on the more specifically cultural aspects, and are inclined to make a virtue out of incompetence. Culturally, that is in regard to basic values and the like, it may be more just to postulate that all humans are equal. With culture in the narrower sense excluded, however, the entire verdict of underdevelopment, and the vision of reality underlying it, begin to come loose at the seams. If culture cannot be taken into consideration, where does a verdict as to developed or underdeveloped apply and where does it not?

Nor is this all. The uneasiness just signalled is aggravated from various quarters. One could draw up a long list, but it will suffice to quote two instances.

The ambiguity of westernization

In good ethnocentric fashion, Westerners tend to equate development in non-Western parts of the world with so-called westernization. In fact, this is done with considerable frequency and ease. Even so, this tendency hurts itself against some hard facts. Let it be true that a considerable part of the stirrings affecting the non-Western parts of the world can be attributed to the Western impact, then yet this provides no excuse for disregarding the equally basic fact that this impact is essentially ambivalent. One of the fundamental reasons why development is such a terribly difficult and erratic business is precisely this ambivalence. Any adoption of things Western is primarily if not exclusively instrumental towards its opposite: self-realization regardless of the West. Conversely, any attempt at self-realization of emergent or resurgent sociocultural entities in the "third world" occurs in the teeth of conditions of one-world interdependence which, in their turn, are largely determined by the Western presence and even to an extent by Western imponderables, whether of the Euro-American or of the Soviet variant. In brief, he who equates development with westernization sees only one face of the coin and is blind to the other.

Complementary hereto, another consideration demands attention: less of an eye-catcher perhaps, but equally important. There is an increasing awareness amongst Western scholars that the Western specificity derives to an extent from being an exception to the rule; the rule in its turn appearing under such names as Common Human Pattern.[2] This is an

---

[2] The term stems from Jan Romein. Comp. his "The Common Human Pattern: Origin and Scope of Historical Theories", *Journ. World Hist.* 4/2 (1958),

intriguing and sophisticated idea, discussion of which falls outside the present scope. Its signal element for present purposes is the inherent reversal of viewpoint. According to this view, the universe is not conceived in the usual way, namely from a vantage point provided and at the same time conditioned by specifically Western modes of perception. Contrariwise, the attempt is to conceive it from a vantage point supposedly reflecting a world-wide mode of perception. This – largely hypothetical – world-wide, common human mode of perception (the common human pattern producive of, or reflecting in, a universe as postulated thereby) in its turn results from the postulate that the West presents an exception. Thus phrased, this surely is an unfinished thought, witness its circular nature. It raises a question that it may not be ready to answer, namely what then is specific to the common human pattern as a vantage point from which to perceive (not to say construct) the universe. Even so, it has the considerable merit of tying in with one-world conceptions befitting present-day conditions. Moreover, it does so in a manner that is fully adequate to expose Western ethnocentrism as something that, even if natural, is open to challenge.

Western role in world demands reconsideration

At this point, we are in a position to draw one provisional conclusion. As Tinbergen [3] and others have been arguing for some time, the Western role in regard to development is up for reconsideration. Truman's Point Four started from premises that, in retrospect, were already obsolete by the time he pronounced it. And along with the Western role, also the Western self-view of this role is up for reconsideration: whether as a model for the non-West to conform to or as a leader for the non-West to follow. Moreover, there is an increasing awareness that in the overall change affecting the world at large, the West is definitely not in the position of being the one invariant. It is worth recalling that if there are nowadays fundamental doubts as regards the Western role and self-view, these are the doubts, primarily if not exclusively, of Westerners. Surely, the non-West tends to be rather vociferous in its doubts on the matter, but upon closer consideration these doubts prove secondary,

p. 449 ff. For a recent discussion comp. W. F. Wertheim, *East-West Parallels, Sociological Approaches to Modern Asia* (The Hague, Van Hoeve, 1964).
[3] J. Tinbergen *et al., Shaping the World Economy, Suggestions for International Economic Policy* (New York, Twentieth Century Fund, 1962). The title of Pt. I, "The World and the West", recalls A. Toynbee's study under the same title (London, Oxford U.P., 1953).

being part of the conditions of ambivalence already signalled. Let it be added furthermore that if this doubt does not facilitate it certainly liberates. It exposes as false any argument to the effect that *les jeux sont faits,* as would have had to be the ultimate conclusion to be drawn from the ethnocentric line of argument, had this been upheld. For development there is neither a necessary model nor a necessary guide. On the contrary, what proves necessary is to reconsider the entire situation.

3

ONE WORLD A-MAKING

One of the realizations that are crucial to this reconsideration refers to
the emergent phenomenon usually called, in Wilkie's phrase, One
World.[1] Unfortunately the somewhat emotional, moralizing way in
which this matter was first presented has tended to persist up to the
present. This may have hampered public opinion in taking cognizance,
in a factually correct manner, of the changes involved, and in drawing
the appropriate conclusions. For present purposes it is useful to start
out from the assertion that primarily, the emergence of the development
problem is symptomatic of the emergence of One World. Nothing is as
illustrative in the connection as the strange fact that any colony upon
achieving independence appears on the world scene as an underdeveloped country. This is, no doubt, partly a matter of terminology (and as
such a valid explanation for the relative lack of alarm with which public
opinion has received it); but at the same time it has profound significance (so profound, indeed, that public opinion may have failed to grasp
it so soon).

Factors of one world

Numerous factors must have played a role in bringing about the state of
affairs that we label as One World. Let me single out three for special
consideration, on account of their particular relevance to the present
subject.

The technological impact

First, technology, especially as referring to transportation and other
kinds of communication. It has effectively altered the human significance of time and place, the two vital dimensions of the human universe. In consequence, the bottom has fallen away from beneath any

[1] Wendell L. Willkie, *One World* (British Publishers' Guild, 1943).

and every construct designed to uphold the solipsism of any existing sociocultural entity. Ethnocentrism, having always necessarily been a myth but having through the millennia proven tenable without undue effort at falsification of reality, faces a crisis. Since quite recently no one can uphold it as a philosophy without constantly having to face brutal proof that he is wrong.

In further consequence, the plurality of human perceptions of the universe – or to put it more briefly and not less correctly, the plurality of human universes, each corresponding to a particular sociocultural (or, for that matter, economico-political) entity, has become problematic in an entirely novel manner. No longer is it enough if people find and uphold a way of (deprecatingly) accounting for the fact that other people exist (with their own universes) who are not intrinsically part of "the" (= "our" own) universe. And this is not all. On top of this, they have to find ways and means to effectively implement the inevitable, vital interdependence that has come to obtain between themselves (that is, their own sociocultural entity, their own "world") and (that of) others, aliens. There is no accepted and reliable way of doing this trick. Any pre-established patterns or models are inapplicable simply on account of being pre-established: they are obsolete. But due to their ready availability and to people's inclination to go on using them, it is hard to do what yet is the only sensible thing to do: consider the position with an open and imaginative mind.

The obsolescence of Western empires

Secondly, note the withering away of the great Western-type empires. Checkered patterns of power, they used to exist in mutual competition. Each embraced bits and pieces of territory, scattered throughout large parts of the world, and controlled these from a centre located somewhere in Europe.

The emergence of these empires, along with their mutual competition, is characteristically Western. It responds to an inner urge towards self-realization and self-vindication through meeting (and to that purpose, seeking) the challenge of "the other".[2] Basically, this is ethnocentrism once over again. But instead of accounting for the alien's existence by negating him, or what is basically the same, deprecating him, it accounts

---

[2] Note that there is a contrary urge that could be said to stand in a complementarity relationship to the one discussed here: "opting out". *Clochards* and hippies offer unwelcome but adequate illustration. So did, in their own manner, various utopian groups and also individuals like Gauguin. So did, vicariously, the author and particularly the readers of works like *Robinson Crusoe*.

for him by reducing him to an instrumental role within the framework of a process of self-vindication. Process that, thereby, necessarily acquires the additional trait of self-expansion. Seldom has expansionism, as the motive force for empire building, been so deeply rooted.[3] The creation of empires of dominance responds primarily to an inner, fundamental urge of the West proper.

In the same manner, the eventual withering away of these empires, of which we are nowadays witnessing the final stages in Aden, Gibraltar and the like, is basically a matter of inner necessity. The gradual but inevitable intensification of control over dominated areas (reinforced, by way of coincidence, by the spread of philosophies that in their turn are offshoots of much the same urges that caused this expansionism) has inexorably necessitated an increasingly active involvement of those dominated. This has engendered a gradual reversal of roles in the dominance relationship.[4] Rationalized and verbalized in inevitably one-sided manner, this has resulted in the irresistible urge towards independence for those hitherto dominated. This has engendered a gradual shift of roles in the relationship of domination. As regards this shift, one has to distinguish between what it might, and perhaps should, have been and that which it has actually become.

Reversal of roles: the wrong outcome

What it has become is close to a reversal of roles. Those hitherto dominated have become independent and amongst them the inner core (of the nationalist movement concerned) have tended to assume the dominant role. In the manner in which they have done so, they have been

[3] Compare, for example, the expansionism inherent in the classical desert empires of the Middle East. By and large, this was rooted in the self-maintenance of authority as a conflict-manipulating device. Thus, the inner necessity mentioned above could but present itself incidentally (namely according to the emergence of conflicts) not persistently. Comp. my "The Tribal Sector in Middle Eastern Society: A Profile", *Corresp. d'Orient: Études*, 5-6 (Bruxelles, 1964), pp. 39-62.

[4] Anticipating the terms of the reasoning that is to follow, one could even argue that the original role division whereby the colonizers gradually conceive of themselves as *ex officio* change agents, and of the dominated population as being in need of change, in other words as changees, has shifted in such a manner that regardless of the role of the colonizers (who insisted on appearing as invariants rather than as covariants), those colonized turned out to be change agents in their own right. A contemporary US parallel is the growing decision of certain socio-economically underprivileged groups, usually indicated by racial names, to become change agents in their own right after having concluded that no benefit is to be gained from continuing in the role of changee, in the hands and at the mercy of change agents holding on to basically obsolete ideas.

hard put to avoid all traces of the previous pattern of domination. The role of the dominated has tended to fall, at times, to those previously dominant and particularly those of the previously dominated category who had been closely associated with them. Nationalizations and sequestrations of property are symptomatic for this tendency. More often, however, this role has simply been continued for the original incumbents: the masses of the populations concerned. No doubt, the crucial moment in this complex process is clearly the urge towards independence in the fullest, strictest sense of the word: an urge that as such is a typical product of the internal secretion of colonial systems.

On the other hand, that which the domination relationship might have developed into is something entirely different. It might have become – and, but for the independence urge, should have become – a continued relationship in which the crucial characteristic should have been changed: effective interdependence instead of dominance-*cum*-dependence. This idea has in fact been presented in various cases when a colony was about to become independent. In no case has this presentation sorted any effect. The French Union, the Netherlands Kingdom new style, they have all proved stillborn. In retrospect it is easy to see that the very wordings in which the idea was presented could but conspire with the worsened relationships of the moment and with the momentary need for spectacular change, to let the pendulum swing to the other extreme. A further element in this "conspiracy" of adverse factors is the non-availability of a valid frame of reference. Again in retrospect, it is abundantly clear that not the pre-existent empires in their decay, but in fact the One World as a living reality should have served as the framework within which to conceive of the status of newly decolonized peoples. Only with such a framework as a given datum, could it have made sense to think of interdependence as really important and to try to make it operational. If such a conception of the world was not entirely lacking, it certainly was ineffective as yet. We must not forget that the colonial empires have at no occasion even come near to appearing as constituents of One World. Much rather, they tended to make up something that one could perhaps call the plural world. Considerable territories, including a universe in its own right like China, have escaped from fully effective dominance by a Western power. More important, if there has been something like a basic unity of outlook underlying the activities of the several Western powers, this unity has never had a chance of effectuation, due to the equally inherent, and at least equally strong, element of mutual competition. It is tempting to venture the suggestion that perhaps at no time have the Western empires exerted so common an impact on the world as a whole, as when they were *in extremis*. But even then, this common impact was unfit to serve as a challenge eliciting a concerted response.

When the colonial empires got into the act of organizing each its part of the world, they did so in response to their own inner urges and to the extent to which parts of the world yielded to their activities. The crucial phenomenon, in the connection, is what Malek Bennabi [5] has called colonizability. Insofar as parts of the world have yielded to the Western impact this was a matter of allowing the latitude in which the Western powers, always competing with one another, could move. It was not because the world at large had a distinct need of large-scale politico-economic organization. But it is precisely this need that, in waning, the colonial empires bequeathed to the world as a whole. The question, upon the demise of the colonial empires, is thus who are the successors that can cope with this need.

The unmet need for a conception of the world as a whole

There can be no doubt whether this question was adequately raised. It was crucial in the reorganization of League of Nations into United Nations. However, the terms in which it was dealt with showed more than their fair share of carry-over from the past. In regard to the matter of how to cope with the need just signalled, there was a blind adherence to inherited concepts of the past, whose obsolete nature has escaped attention due to the inevitably distorted value system that had guided warfare during World War II. Independence was something sacred in those days, and there appears to have been no effective questioning whether independence and sovereignty of nation-states are or are not synonymous.

In consequence, the pattern of politico-economical and even perhaps cultural relationships that was to become the signal feature of the new One World, was inevitably conceived starting out from the sovereign state-nation as its basis. With the wisdom of hindsight, we are painfully aware now that this was an inadequate and even false basis, but that is how it went.

In practice, this meant that the crucial question just mentioned boiled down to the very different question who were candidates to succeed the defunct colonial empires and how would they, if successful in their claims, go about imposing some sort of pattern on the world as a whole.

[5] Malek Bennabi, *Vocation de l'Islam* (Paris, Seuil, 1954).

The two main victorious powers, easily falling into their post-war role of The Big Powers, whilst anxious to avoid the semblance of imperialism, were eager to play the role of world organizers but basically uncertain about the manner in which to do so. For one thing, they had not merely inherited the mutual competition of their predecessors, but also the inner necessity to confront the outside world on their own terms. No doubt, these urges were very much at odds with whatever realization there may have existed concerning the need for a new world order. Thus, whatever possibilities the situation contained were spoiled within little time, and by the time people found their bearings again it was within an apparently senseless framework, duly provided with an equally senseless name: the Cold War. This war, *n'en déplaise* President de Gaulle, is still on.

In their turn, the small powers and the powerless states, new or not so new, were in no position to contribute much towards a new world formula, nor did they have much to contribute beyond anxious trepidation. In the case of the new nations, their very emergence was a matter of international, formal recognition prior to becoming a matter of internal, effective crystallization. Accordingly, there was a tendency to find, and expose, neo-colonialism and neo-imperialism. A good deal of this resulted simply from the circumstance that those concerned were in no condition to make allowance for the absence of novel formulas whilst passing their verdicts on activities still shaped according to obsolete ones. The point is that for lack of alternatives even the most sincere attempt to contribute to a new world order geared to interdependence had, and still has, to rely for a major or lesser extent on obsolete forms. Moreover, those who are loud in their incriminations tend to overlook that their own adherence to national sovereignty is open to the same criticisms.

The impact of obsolete paradigms

It was inevitable in the preceding section to anticipate to a considerable extent what really belongs in the present one. Still in connection with the emergence of One World, a third signal phenomenon is the backlash of obsolete concepts and models. It is equally visible, and equally important, amongst new nations as amongst the established ones. And as regards the former, it is as much of a distorting factor in the response, given in many parts of the world, to the so-called impact of the West, as it is in the processes currently labelled decolonization, modernization and the like.

In order to elaborate this point somewhat, it is convenient to begin by resuming some remarks already made. An appropriate sequel to the withering away of the colonial empires could have been the emergence of patterns of effective interdependence between entities that could, clearly, not have been defined as sovereign nations but that, in the same process, should in their turn have been created or redefined. In and insofar as there has been a tendency in this direction, it has been obliterated under the backlog of inherited and for all practical purposes obsolete "paradigms".

There are those who have attempted to argue that independence must be understood as a necessary intermediate stage, a preparatory move towards interdependence. This may be so, but only to an extent. It is at least equally true that independence, the way people cling to it and in fact believe in it, is nothing short of a relapse into ideas and constructs that, if measured by contemporary standards, are not merely obsolete but in fact disastrous. They represent a revival, in unholy unison, of the particular ethnocentrisms of the emerging nation states of 17th and 18th century Europe and those of closed community living in many other parts of the world. The jealously guarded sovereignty of new – and of some older – nations is sacred in the original Latin, fully ambiguous sense of the word *sacer*. Worse, it is strictly self-purposive and bent upon self-perpetuation. Rather than heralding interpendence, independence may nip it in the bud.

Non-Westerners have felt increasingly urged to do two mutually contradictory things at once: emulate the West and eliminate it. It must be regarded as a case of brilliant economizing that often the same means have been made serviceable to both goals. Ideas and ideals, in being adopted, proved at the same time valuable weapons for combat. Thus, for example, human dignity, democracy, liberty. Most famous and most ominous example: nationality. These and other imponderables, along with more visible and material goods, were transferred from one culture context to another with more consideration for possibilities to apply them than for the desirability that they should somehow fit in their new context. Neo-nationalism therefore tends to be at least as solipsistic, as overheated as European nationalisms in their heyday; at the same time it may elicit far less romantic belief amongst the leaders, and be quite hazardously founded on the historical and geographical conditions of the place and time concerned. This is a bad thing in itself. It is worse because, like property in an earlier day, nationality, particularly in the form of national sovereignty, is manifestly in need of careful reconsideration, both as a concept and for its actual practice.[6]

The nation-state is on probation

Under present conditions, nation-states old and new, large and small, are not merely *ad hoc* like all human existence is. They are effectively and emphatically on probation. Once again, this is basically a problem of obsolete models and patterns by means of which people try to cope with a novel situation. This is partly because nothing better is available, partly because many are hesitant to recognize a need for new conceptual tools by which to deal with novel conditions.

This being so, the study of sociocultural entities, particularly the ones of optimal size and scope, acquires a new and critical significance. It is necessary once more to study them in their conceptual as well as in their operational aspects, both in regard to determinants of the identity of each and in regard to the necessary interaction between ever variable numbers of them. Now this may sound like forcing an open door. Nothing could appear more natural than that the upsurging tide of studies in nation building [7] and institution building, along with the vogue of sys-

---

[6]   The parallel is quite interesting. It could perhaps be argued that property is under certain circumstances a signal feature of personal or individual identity, and in the same manner sovereignty is under certain circumstances a signal feature of the identity of sociocultural entities comprising plural human individuals. Of the latter entities, the nation-state is only one example. For particular periods and places, the family or the tribe could serve as equally good illustrations.

[7]   There is a swelling tide of publications on this subject. Some examples: American Academy of Political and Social Science, The Annals, *New Nations, The Problem of Political Development* (New York, Random House, March 1965), vol. 358; David E. Apter, *The Politics of Modernization* (Chicago, U.P., 1965); Reinhard Bendix, *Nation-Building and Citizenship, Studies of Our Changing Social Order* (New York, Wiley, 1964); C. E. Black, *The Dynamics of Modernization, A Study in Comparative History* (New York, Harper Row, 1966); Karl W. Deutsch and William J. Foltz (eds.), *Nation Building* (New York, Atherton, 1966); Amitai Etzioni, *Political Unification, A Comparative Study of Leaders and Forces* (New York, Holt Reinehard Winston, 1965); Jason L. Finkle and Richard W. Gable (eds.), *Political Development and Social Change* (New York, Wiley, 1966); Philip E. Jacob and James V. Toscano (eds.), *The Integration of Political Communities* (Philadelphia, Lippincott, 1964); J. P. Nettl, *Political Modernization* (London, Faber and Faber, 1967); Dankwart A. Rustow, *A World of Nations, Problems of Political Modernization* (Washington, D.C., Brookings Inst., 1967); K. H. Silvert (ed.), *Expectant Peoples, Nationalism and Development* (New York, Random House: Vintage, 1963); Myron Weiner (ed.), *Modernization, The Dynamics of Growth* (New York, Basic Books, 1966); Claude E. Welch Jr. (ed.), *Political Modernization* (Belmont, Calif., Wadsworth, 1967).

tems analysis,[8] whatever the term may mean, should meet this demand. Could anything more be needed, at the present stage, but some careful warning concerning the dangers of too easy an affirmation of the nation-state as the paradigm for present and future developments? [9]

There is indeed occasion for some caution. The need for analysis of whole sociocultural entities will, in fact, not necessarily be met by much that nowadays attracts attention. In too many cases the level of abstraction maintained is inadequate for the purpose.

Along with the facts studied, too much of the analytical categories employed remains *situé* et *daté*. This is particularly true of a considerable number of recent American studies in modernization and nation building. Even though they are clearly inspired by the shock of realization that to speak of such things as the need to democratize betrays ethnocentrism, they have not always moved very much beyond the formal avoidance of some verbal pitfalls.

[8] A work to be discussed further below is Bertram H. Gross, *The State of the Nation, Social Systems Accounting* (London, Tavistock, 1966). See also Z. Klausner (ed.), *The Study of Total Societies* (Garden City, N.Y., Doubleday: Anchor, 1967). For a summing-up of sociological theory in the connection, comp. Walter Buckley, *Sociology and Modern Systems Theory* (Englewood Cliffs, N.Y., Prentice Hall, 1967).

[9] For some further suggestions on this subject see my *The Nation and the Ideal City* (The Hague, Mouton, 1967). Comp. also Ernest B. Haas, *Beyond the Nation State* (Stanford, U.P., 1964); W. J. M. Mackenzie, *Politics and Social Science* (Harmondsworth, Penguin, 1967); John W. Spanier, *World Politics in an Age of Revolution* (New York, Praeger, 1967).

PART II

FOUR QUESTIONS CONCERNING DEVELOPMENT

4

THE UNIT OF DEVELOPMENT

These features of the emerging One World form the perspective in which one has to consider development. To such consideration, there appear to be at least five different crucial issues. They refer to the entity going through development, the nature of development, the scope of development, control over development and evaluation of development. On each point, some observations are to follow.

An unfounded assumption: the nation-state as the natural unit of development

In the light of what was said thus far, there is reason to ask which is the sociocultural and/or politico-economical entity going through development. As stated, the current assumption is that the nation-state is the natural unit of development. But here and there, some doubts or afterthoughts are beginning to be heard.

In the West, statehood as a form of organization for political and to an extent also economic power, and nationhood as a form of organization for social and to an extent cultural cohesion of human groupings, have merged at a given point in time, in such a manner as to afford a procedure for the distribution of control over public affairs. The merger, significantly, has no name of its own and is referred to now as nation and then as state, sometimes as country and sometimes as people.[1] If under the circumstances there was concern about the viability of the new formula, it was obfuscated in one out of two ways. Either it took shape as considerations of an enthousiastic, idealistic nature. Or it took shape as systematic theorizing and philosophizing: this is the period when the social sciences were born. In either case, the net effect is support and vindication for the new type of social organization.

---

[1] The mutuality of perspective between people and country, more exactly between locality and inhabitants, as mutually defining one another, is a recognized fact since millennia. Often, one name indicates both.

In consequence of Western expansion, partial replicas of this pattern have been superimposed, in various parts of the world, on entirely different structures. Gradual, but none-too-complete, obsolescense of the latter, and unintended use of the former toward newly emerging responses to the Western impact, have resulted in the phenomenon already discussed: an avalanche of adoptions of the nation-state model to suit the needs of the "new states" (more precisely, of many newly emerging sociocultural and/or economico-political entities bent upon achieving self-realization, primarily through formal international recognition). The inevitable consequence is a viability problem in quite many cases, sometimes more, sometimes less acute.

It thus becomes clear that there is indeed reason for doubts and afterthoughts as to the assumption, only too natural for economics, that the nation-state is the natural unit of development.

The crucial point in the connection is not always clearly distinguished, and indeed seldom considered for its full implications. When it does attract attention, it tends to feature as the problem of territoriality. As a matter of historical coincidence, the Western nation-state, upon emerging, was territorially fixed. (This was the more or less natural continuation of geographical fixation of rights and privileges, vested in persons or bodies in earlier days.) The consequence is that contemporary Westerners in their thinking about larger sociocultural units are inclined to take territorial fixation for granted, as a natural precondition. How far this kind of culture conditioning goes appears dramatically whenever territoriality, in being discussed for its own sake, is presented as fully natural. This sort of legitimation can be seen carried to its extreme in the work of R. Ardrey,[2] who vindicates territoriality in human affairs by the not uncommon, though fundamentally inconclusive, procedure of arguing that it is commonly found in animal life as well. The difficulty in his argument is that what he describes as territoriality is not necessarily a principle of life; nor are the variants he describes necessarily a matter of territorial fixation of human or animal existence as a matter of principle. In order to achieve a more careful appreciation of the matter it is not even necessary to draw upon the animal realm. Anthropological study of human groups reveals that there is a significant and traceable relationship between three variables, namely size and structure of human group, nature of human action in regard to the part of the earth serving as its habitat, and human conception of the relationship between humans and their geographical *locus*. Studies

[2]   R. Ardrey, *The Territorial Imperative* (New York, Atheneum, 1966).

undertaken for example in North Africa by experts like J. Berque and P. Bourdieu [3] underscore the entirely variable, and on this account sometimes elusive, nature of this latter relationship. This refers not merely to variable location in the case of nomads and semi-nomads. It particularly refers to the sketchy definition (*e.g.*, terms of rights, whether group rights or individual rights) that the relationship receives, and, for that matter, needs. So far as definition occurs it may assume contractual form rather than anything else (the *khammesat* being a good North-African example: the sedentary tenant sharecropper working and thereby holding land that is thus implicitly demonstrated to belong to certain nomads). The conclusion is that territorial fixation is by no means a *conditio sine qua non* for human group life, not even for the largest group, but rather a matter of coincidence. Contemporary Westerners who think otherwise are subject to an optical illusion: in normal ethnocentric fashion they take their own present situation to be general and normal.

Surely, the trend nowadays throughout the world is for territorial definition and fixation. This is perhaps to an extent a matter of spreading Western ideas; more importantly, it is perhaps an inevitable corrolary of increased interaction between human groups which elicits increased definition, also territorially, of their respective identities. But if this seems to enhance the identification of group with territory, it yet does not alter the fact that territorial fixation is not a primary datum of human existence.

It is this realization that one must bring to bear when considering whether the territorially fixed nation-state is necessarily and inevitably the natural unit for development: that is, in the last resort, whether it is the natural unit encompassing human life in all its aspects. Considering the matter in this light, it appears correct to expect that even if there may be more of an urge towards territorial fixation under contemporary conditions than there may have existed under different conditions, it yet remains undecided whether such territorial fixation should be total. It remains an open question whether omnipurpose human groups, called nation-states, would necessarily exist in sovereignty: that is, in effective mutual entrenchment (although contiguously), within manifest and effective territorial limits. Indeed, upon closer consideration this would seem neither natural nor necessary.

On the contrary, it appears much more likely that human groups, defined not in comprehensive omnipurpose fashion but rather in terms

[3] Such as the latter's *Sociologie de l'Algérie* (Paris, P.U.F., 1958).

of some particular specificity and thus in limited-purpose fashion, would each have their own limitations, some more some less clearly manifest territorially within nation-states. This pattern is too well known to need any description. In the Netherlands, provinces exist side by side with *polders* (water control units); whilst clearly distinct in terms of jurisdiction and purposes, they are territorially defined regardless of one another. The example can be enlarged and complicated a thousandfold. The point is that there appears to be no valid reason why a pattern composed of such plural, territorially variable, and variously defined human units should, at a certain moment in time and at a certain (but quite variable) order of magnitude, be interrupted brusquely in favour of a contrasting pattern, providing allegedly all-purpose frames of reference, called the nation-state. The shift from the one pattern to the other was comprehensible and perhaps inevitable at a time when communications were such that large empires, not nearly embracing the world as a whole, topped off a number of lesser, variously defined units. But such empires were always limited-purpose propositions, and necessarily so. So far as omnipurpose units existed, they were the very small ones, of relatively secluded face-to-face living: the village, the tribal nucleus. The trouble with the nation-state is that it constitutes an attempt to match the omnipurpose nature of the one kind of unit with the size of the other, under conditions when neither of the two are viable without profound modification. Yet, the tendency of the Western nation-state is nowadays to become increasingly self-purposive and to become an effective force in ever more aspects of human existence. The same tendency, even less effectively hampered by tradition, is visible in the newly independent states. If this is understandable on many counts, one must yet keep in mind two considerations. One is that in its ultimate totalitarian implications it risks becoming pernicious to human dignity and freedom. The other is that insofar as it could enhance a development effort, this effort, unlike development proper, is necessarily a limited-purpose, never an omnipurpose affair: so that there is fundamental, usually disregarded, disparity between the omnipurpose nation-state and the development effort that it embodies. This discrepancy is not merely dangerous in the way just described, it also constitutes a severe drawback for the efficacy of the effort just mentioned.

It must therefore be hoped that before long the already noticeable trend away from maximization of the nation-state will gather more impetus. If so, a broad and not suddenly interrupted range of sizes and scopes of human units could come into their own: as a perhaps less simple but in many ways both more human and more efficient pattern of world-wide crystallization and institutionalization of human togetherness. Accordingly, one would look forward to relatively small units for political participation, feeding into larger ones for co-ordination of political decision making; but at the same time one would look for relatively larger units for, say, purposes of economic planning. In Europe, for example, one can distinguish economic regions that have remarkably little to do with existing political boundaries.[4]

Alternative units as the frame of reference for development

In the Middle East, the ambivalence between Arabism on the one hand and nationalism (in terms of the states that have succeeded the mandates) on the other proves a major drawback. In Africa, the competitive attractions of tribalism, nationalism and Africanism illustrate the same fundamental lack of a self-evident frame of reference for development. And is it a matter of chance that economists are tentatively beginning to think in polycentric and regionalist terms, that is, in terms of possible alternatives to the nation-state as the only frame of reference for their theory-building and policy-designing?[5] For the nation-state to be upheld as the natural unit of development, it is not enough that statehood is the official requirement for world-wide recognition.[6]

Persistence of the nation-state as the unit of development

One of the reasons why everybody can afford to keep referring to the nation-state is that the meaning of the term has, in the course of time, been stretched to suit convenience. But it has been stretched so far that as a natural frame of reference for development its use has become problematic. The common assumption is that humans develop in togetherness as nations. This is doubtful for various reasons already discussed. It is also dangerous, any time the state would consequently appear as the agent of development in addition to being its frame of reference. Then, a government is bound to feature as the monopolist of development and the nation as a passive category submitting to

[4] Comp. F. Compagna, *L'Europa delle Regioni* (Napoli, Ed. Sci. Ital., 1964).
[5] On polycentric planning see Rudolf Bićanić, *Problems of Planning, East and West* (The Hague, Mouton, 1967). On regional planning, see J. G. M. Hilhorst, *Regional Development Theory, An Attempt to Synthesize* (The Hague, Mouton, 1967). The disadvantage of polycentric as compared to regional planning would seem to be that it provides less occasion to reconsider the one-sidedness of the current fashion for mathematical economics based entirely on a rather frightening form of reductionism, namely quantification.
[6] *United Nations Charter*, Ch. II., Artt. 3, 4: members must be states.

development: which is about as vicious a contradiction in terms as one could ever expect to meet.

He who accepts that the nation-state cannot possibly be the one natural frame of reference for development is bound to face up to the question concerning other units of development. Of course, one can opt for the easy solution and refer to units like the community or the region as alternatives, some of long standing. It is clear, however, that this can merely shift the question: how many possible frames of reference are there, which are the more promising ones?

The unit of development: the matter of homogeneity and diffraction

The crucial consideration, in this connection, refers back once more to the impact, already mentioned, of changes in the spatiotemporal frame of existence and to the concomitant urge towards participation or interaction. More specifically, it concerns the nature and impact of communications media. Communication nowadays is characterized by nothing so much as relative independence from both time and space. The signal feature in both regards is proximity. Besides, there are fundamental shifts in the appeal of communication media on man's perceptive apparatus and on his involvement.

Thinking more or less along some of the lines developed by McLuhan,[7] one begins to see that certain characteristics that would apply to the natural unit of development if considered according to standards hitherto prevalent (and no doubt derived from Western developments of the relatively recent past: and those considered, in good ethnocentric fashion, as general and categorical), may have lost or be losing their validity. Particularly affected by recent developments would appear to be the characteristic of integration through homogenization, and its sequel of unlimited expansiveness.

These indeed are signal features of the West during the last two centuries or so. They connote a universe for which the development urge is basic. It is somehow curious, given the roots of the word, that the term democracy should have played such a central role in the thinking devoted to the matter by those concerned. Indeed the belief in its necessity is firmly rooted in that most irrational of rational creeds, the pre-established harmony as preached by liberalism. Whatever differentiation, diffraction, potential or even actual conflict may occur is essentially

[7] Marshall McLuhan, *Understanding Media: The Extensions of Man* (New York, New American Library: Signet, 1964), pp. 47 f., 59, 75, 89, 92, 156, 204, 267, 270, 274 ff., 280 f., 299.

instrumental towards ever more and further homogenization (this being the current form of integration). Conflict is, at root, nothing but an occasion for creative conflict resolution. The universe moves towards synthesis, the classless state, to self-propelled growth in the matter of (mainly material) means to satisfy human needs. McLuhan's one and only explanatory device in considering all this is the nature of available media of information (and his term information is extremely broad, easily including relationships as such and any variety of wealth and control). To him, the alphabet and the written word are symptomatic, and decisive, for the universe now under consideration. However, things are on the move. The new media are, in fact, a new universe, even though people are slow to perceive it and to draw the consequences.

For all practical purposes, the very homogeneity and expansiveness that were crucial traits hitherto (because, one may add, they were the means to meet the inherent weaknesses of the communications system as a self-propelling pattern) are no longer indispensable. Accordingly, the diffraction and differentiation of sociocultural reality need no longer to be dealt with in such a manner as to forestall their potentially dangerous implications.

In a way, man can now better afford to take them for what they are, namely necessary corollaries of the complexity (and that is basically, the comprehensiveness) of human sociocultural existence. He is in a position to perceive them, and accordingly to deal with them, as positive modalities of the manifestation of his universe. The plural nature of sociocultural reality is no longer necessarily problematic or even potentially pernicious, the way it is to the ethnocentric mind.

For all practical purposes, this novel perception would seem to entail a new opportunity for non-homogeneity, in other words for the effective functioning of non-optimal and non-expansive sociocultural entities, to feature as the building material for the human universe. The prospect is the more important as it appears to be the only one within which the One World, both as a notion and as an actual state of affairs, need not cause insuperable difficulties for thought and action.

The point is that in the light of this prospect one obtains more than a mere confirmation of the already known fact that the optimal if not maximal, expansive universe, as exemplified through the ages in various kinds of empires and more recently in the Western expansive (colonialist or imperialist) nation-state, is obsolete. More important, one begins to see that it has no need to continue in its role as the main or primary sociocultural entity. Also important is that this in itself hopeful fact need not connote the thoroughly frightening prospect for which Mc-Luhan seems to warn us at times, namely a relapse in some sort of world-wide tribalism. True, the danger is there. Tribalism is nothing but the closed universe of ethnocentrism in smallest compass. Thanks to the new media, it could exist in widest compass. There is some risk that notwithstanding the withering away of the homogenous expansive sociocultural entity of predominantly ethnocentric self-perception, ethno-centrism could survive, as a kind of free-floating poison. In fact, some of its forebodings are visible with uncanny clarity in today's neo-nationalisms. On the other hand, there is no reason to exclude the possibility that ethnocentrism would somehow be reduced to its proper proportions rather than being blown up to extreme proportions in the processes now under way. The increasingly complex and in fact plural-istic modalities of man's involvement in sociocultural entities of various kinds and sizes could be hoped to prevent his undue fixation, in ethno-centric manner, on one, to the exclusion of any others.

Increased interaction on basis of complexity

No doubt, the very complexity of this prospective state of affairs is bound to imply questions concerning integration. But the kind of inte-gration one would have to envisage would not come as a categorical imperative operating through homogenization-*cum*-expansiveness. Rather, it is likely to come about much more on an *ad hoc* basis, with interaction rather than homogenization as its main operative device. In the same way, one anticipates intensification of relationships of mutual relevance between entities to take the place held by expansiveness as a necessity in the now obsolete state of affairs.

Plural and variable units of development: the operational view

So far, it may appear as if we are indulging in speculation about remote and entirely vague prospects, the urgency of McLuhan's message not-withstanding. But even he who insists on keeping his feet on the ground cannot miss all the signs and fail to see the practical importance of what was just argued. What this prospect means in practice is that the natural units of development are necessarily various both in kind and size, perhaps relatively small rather than necessarily optimal, internally complex rather than homogenous and externally bent upon interaction rather than expansive. Considered in this light, it is no matter of sheer chance that community development survives notwithstanding its basical-ly wrong philosophy (dealing with the community by itself, that is in isolation rather than in interaction) and its relative lack of success. Nor could it be a matter of simple coincidence that co-operatives, communes, party cells, and the like, come more and more to the forefront as the places where the real action is. What is largely missing, on the other hand, is the understanding why this should be so. One expects, however, that as time progresses more people will see more clearly in this regard.

Anticipating somewhat the discussion, below, on control over development, one interesting consequence may be pointed out. With units of development of various kinds and sizes, perhaps even of various levels of organization, simultaneously effective, the modalities of integration are likely to appear as a more or less diffuse egalitarianism. A pattern of interaction that, considered from another angle, will appear as co-ordination. Not authoritative homogenizing co-ordination but co-ordination as service rendered. Translating this into terms of authority one seems to arrive at the expectation that the Big Brother prospect that has sometimes been associated with the advance of the new media is less likely than authority as the clearing house of information and of control over the distribution of information plus ensuing power, wealth etc. The point is that there seems to be less opportunity for authority to become maximized and self-purposive, even though its persistence is likely to prove more marked than might seem likely given the pre-dominance of *ad hoc* relationships in the context in which it would operate. What is overlooked by those who fear the Big Brother prospect is the crucial importance of feed-back for purposes of exertion of authority along the lines here envisaged.

5

THE NATURE OF DEVELOPMENT

The second point that currently, and for the coming years, demands careful attention is the nature of development.

Development: a concept and its meanings

The term development has an intriguing etymological ambivalence that reflects occasionally in some ambivalence of meaning in its current usage. There is an active meaning: development is action in order to make something develop. And there is a medial meaning: something goes through a developmental process. The latter is the more usual of the two. Upon closer inspection, each meaning appears to elicit some fundamental criticism.

The active meaning is sometimes said to have a complement in a passive meaning. Although this is apparently correct, it does not really mean that a third meaning is added to the two just listed. As a matter of principle, the addition has no significance. Everything that can be stated in regard to the active meaning applies to the passive just as well. Practically, however, it has some importance. It helps to bring to the fore some of the things that must be said about both meanings and that risk to be overlooked if one concentrates on the active one only.

The combination of active and passive meanings into one – operational rather than theoretical – complex is typical of the viewpoint of the colonial civil servant and – *bien étonnés de se trouver ensemble* – that of many a social worker. Nothing is quite as illustrative of this viewpoint as the concept of (official) development agent or change agent. This often used term signals the – mostly tacit – assumption that in principle every development situation implies the occurrence of *the* (that is, one, official) development agent as its centrepiece. This assumption is not tenable in practice, and theoretically it is wide open to challenge. In practice, it causes grave difficulty in the matter of the proper identification of various urges, forces or actors, often variously directed if not competing, that occur in one given development situation. For example, in the eyes of certain American social workers or charitable agencies, Negroes could appear, more or less categorically, as "changees". But in the eyes of certain Negro groups or individuals (for instance, the Black Power group), they may very well feature as change agents, whether in regard to the Negro category in particular or American society at large. (Unfortunately, in the same eyes the social worker may appear as ineffective in regard to change if not as opposed to change.)

What is worse, the assumption of the apparent change agent is weak theoretically. Its roots lie in the subject-object dichotomy of days past. It is built on an objectifying approach to reality. This in its turn assumes that a given sociocultural entity can be pure object to action on the part of some distinct agent featuring as pure subject. It has no way of accounting for the (contemporary) realization that, precisely on account of its action-involvement in the "object", a given "subject's" distinctness is only one aspect of a considerably more complex identity, and an incidental one at that. In fact, it echoes the 19th century viewpoint.[1] As will be argued below, a more acceptable conceptualization may be achieved by starting out from a rather more abstract notion like "instance of development". A given instance of development, in this sense, could have various manifestations, including that of change agent and that of changee, plus any combinations of the two.

As regards the medial meaning, the same critique would apply but to a lesser extent. The real difficulty here is its vagueness. For one thing, development is too often a euphemism for un(der)development: the expression of a pious hope as a substitute for the passing of a shattering verdict. For another, there is no conception of reality currently available and of sufficiently wide acceptability that could serve to underpin the concept and thus give it a badly needed dose of theoretical lucidity and practical validity.

Not that such a conception is entirely lacking; in fact, there is reason to believe that, particularly in sociology, we are gradually moving towards it. In order that it become effectively useful, a prior condition has to be met, namely the consummation of a rather fundamental shift in the conception of reality that serves the social sciences as their point of departure. Symptomatic for the traditional view, still current but

---

[1] Jules Monnerot, *Les faits sociaux ne sont pas des choses* (Paris, Gallimard, 1946).

subject to visible obsolescence, is the curious fact that in most sociology texts change is relegated to the final chapter. Symptomatic for its gradual replacement could become the current fashion to give sociology texts titles cast in terms of process or action. The contents may not always come up to the expectations aroused by these titles, but there is no reason why this could not improve.

After all, this is no less than a matter of complete reconceptualization, involving a considerable amount of redefinition of existing terminology or creation of new terminology. The ultimate result could be a conception of sociocultural reality in terms of process. Within such a conceptual framework, change would feature simply as a variant of process and development as a variant of change. More precisely, change would feature as noticed process and development as change with an inherent moment of direction or focussing.[2]

Development: a problem in basic conceptualization

For the purpose of the present argument it seems correct to anticipate the successful completion of these reorientations, and consequently to cast the discussion of the nature of development in terms not yet commonly used and not yet fully articulate. Thus, repeating what was just suggested, our query concerning the nature of development could be answered with the following tentative definition.

Development is a variant of process (the common intelligible appearance of sociocultural reality) that involves perceptibility and an inherent moment of directedness. The circumstances under which it will occur deserve more systematic study than they have received thus far. It will affect sociocultural entities of variable size, and may be particularly perceptible if affecting optimal size entities such as entire empires or nation-states. As regards scope, it will tend to be comprehensive always, but the distribution of accents may vary. (More on this point later.) Within it, one may try to distinguish analytically between entity representing developmental process and (sub-)entity representing developmental impulse, provided one takes care to avoid the trappings of obsolete causality. The only means to do this is the consistent maintenance of a conceptualization in terms of intersubjectivity.

No doubt, all these are ideas badly in need of further clarification

---

[2] For a fuller elaboration of these ideas, comp. my *Society as Process, Intelligible Fields in the Social Sciences* and *Social Scientists in Pursuit of Social Change* (The Hague, Mouton, 1962, 1966, 1967).

and elaboration. For such a purpose, this is not the occasion; nor is it likely to be a one man's job.

The matter of modalities of development

The question concerning the nature of development has a natural complement in the question concerning its modalities.

At a first blush, it could appear as if our present treatment of the subject could hardly cope with a question of this sort, being too broad and too general. Would not modality be primarily a matter of culture conditioning, historical coincidence, geographical peculiarity and the like? Fair enough; but if this is correct, it necessarily applies to the entire argument. Thus in regard to modalities as in regard to nature it appears worth-while to try and ascertain whether some useful insight could be gained: perhaps at a level of abstraction somewhat deeper than spatiotemporal coincidence.

Enlarging scale and increasing participation: a complementarity

What comes to mind in the connection is a complementarity of trends, for neither of which a name is readily available. Relying on existing terminology, one could call the one enlargement of scale and the other increasing participation of the individual in the public sphere.[3] To some, these names are bound to evoke Herbert Spencer's terms homogeneity and heterogeneity.[4] But they differ from his in being neither deterministic nor mechanistic. To a strictly logical viewpoint, the two are virtually contradictory: as befits a complementarity construct. Historically speaking, both can be traced back, to a considerable extent, to the impact of communications technology, already discussed. The enlargement of scale would appear to follow immediately from the increasingly effective means to reduce the effect of distance and time lapse on human action. The increased urge towards participation would seem to reflect the same impulse as interiorized in common awareness of those concerned.[5]

---

[3] This complementary pair reflects, under circumstances of development, the complementarity of what I have elsewhere called synergic and dysergic trends pertaining to process as such. Please refer to titles in preceding note.

[4] Herbert Spencer, *First Principles of a New System of Philosophy* (1862) (New York, De Witt, 1958), p. 394: "Evolution is an integration of matter and concomitant dissipation of motion; during which the matter passes from an indefinite, incoherent homogeneity to a definite, coherent heterogeneity (...)."

[5] The present line of argument is perhaps not too different from that of so-called neo-evolutionists. Comp. Herbert R. Barringer, George I. Blanksten and

Note that nowadays, the complementarity of enlarging scale and increasing participation occurs world-wide, just as development is a world-wide phenomenon. The manifestations may be different as between developing and developed areas, but this cannot exempt the latter from sharing, to the full extent, in what is going on.

Curiously, one sometimes gets the impression that whilst in developed areas these things assume an entirely problematic, almost threatening appearence, they tend to be presented rather more as a challenge in regard to the developing ones: which is perhaps a matter of undue euphemisms to which development experts tend to succumb. As regards the former, it is increasingly fashionable to speak, in quite alarmist terms, of sick culture and the like. Some of the dealings that sociologists have with the matter occur under ominous labels like alienation.[6] Surely, these are entirely valid and even promising approaches: privided one remains aware that they tend to single out one aspect of a considerably wider and more profound problem, the depth and width of which have definitely escaped Hegel, who coined the term alienation, and also Marx, who circulated it.

What matters for present purposes is that the complementarity of enlargement of scale and of urge towards increased participation would appear to constitute a frame of reference within which it should be possible to construct a systematic typological understanding of modalities of development. Insofar as development is a variant, ultimately, of process, the systematics involved should somehow prove to run parallel to the systematics of the analysis, suggested previously, of the operational features of sociocultural entities as such. Insofar as any given sociocultural entity would feature as the context in which development occurs, the modalities of the one can be expected to reflect in those of the other.

Rayfond W. Mack (eds.), *Social Change in Developing Areas, A Reinterpretation of Evolutionary Theory* (Cambridge, Mass., Schenkman, 1965).

[6] Comp. Melvin Seeman, "On the Meaning of Alienation", *ASR*, 24 (Dec. 1959), pp. 783-791. For further references see *idem*, "On the Personal Consequences of Alienation in Work", *Amer. Sociol. Rev.*, 32 (Apr. 1967), pp. 273-285.

6

THE SCOPE OF DEVELOPMENT

Next, consider the scope of development. The term scope, in this connection, is meant to stand for something different than the size of the entity going through development. It is intended to refer to qualitative, not quantitative considerations.

The crucial significance of comprehensiveness

There is an increasing readiness to recognize (and even to act upon the recognition) that development processes are comprehensive not partial. If a given state or society is developing, it develops in every respect: not merely in technology or national income or some combination of a few aspects. In fact, as said above, even culture is somehow involved; and so is any other aspect of the sociocultural, economico-political entity concerned.

As suggested previously, this raises the question of differential accents. The matter, important as it is, is inadequately studied. Some light could perhaps be shed on it, in preparatory fashion, by studies, as suggested before, on the functioning of (optimal) sociocultural entities as such.

For the time being, this question is bound to be obscured somewhat by a preliminary matter. This is the problem of how to account, both in theory and in practice, for the realization that development is fully comprehensive. Interestingly, this realization is brought home in the practice of development work rather than through *a priori* theorizing. Again quite significantly, it comes in the company of two other realizations, both to the effect that certain preconceived ideas, such as progressivism or ethnocentrism, are not tenable. Fascinating as they are, however, these coincidences (by no means a matter of mere chance) present some acute problems.

The implications of comprehensiveness

At the verbal level these problems do not appear insoluble. If, for instance, one tries to envisage the consequences for social scientists, it is not really difficult to recognize that henceforth we must work not as separate disciplines but in multidisciplinary, or perhaps rather inter-disciplinary, fashion. This point will be taken up in a later stage of the argument.

Mutatis mutandis the same applies to development action, sometimes too easily seen (according to a line of reasoning that is obsolete in its turn) as the application of development theory to a given object. In this case, the matter is further bedeviled by the circumstance that insofar as the problem is manifest it will appear as an organizational rather than a fundamental issue. Thus, the comprehensiveness of community development projects, at the "micro" level, and, at the "macro" level, organizational devices as the Greek Ministry of Co-ordination, may be played up as valid ways of coping with the difficulty. With due recognition of the possibility that devices like these may have a beneficial effect, the fundamental question remains whether they constitute adequate responses to the challenge at hand. To this question, no satisfactory answer is as yet available.

7

CONTROL OVER DEVELOPMENT

The fourth crucial issue is control over development. The matter has come up occasionally in preceding remarks, particularly about objectification versus intersubjectivity. This is the moment to pull the various strings together.

Subject versus object: a false dichotomy

Control over development used to be – and to many, is today – a self-evident thing. A state, society or economy is in need of development. Consequently an expert, agency, government, takes action in regard to this economy or society so as to cause it to develop. In so doing the agent of development will attempt to achieve certain goals that he has set with regard to his object of development, whether in agreement with or regardless of those constituting the object of development. Both for purposes of goal-setting and of deciding upon the appropriate means towards set goals, the agent employs a given body of knowledge on which his expert status is founded. This knowledge is, for all practical purposes, pre-established. If in the course of its application it would prove subject to modifications, these could hardly affect the element of persistence in its nature, as compared to the incidental character of its application to a particular case.

This neat picture was perhaps passable, though wide open to challenge, twenty years ago. Nowadays it can at best be considered a relic from past times. The reasons have been summed up already. Knowledge is not objective in the sense of being timeless and placeless, even if it attempts to be general. Nor is it objectifying in the sense that what it takes to change condition X into condition Y, is to apply formula – that is, theory – A or B. Besides, the non-existence of a self-evident, necessary model for development is fully matched by the non-existence of self-evident, necessary leaders towards development, be they experts, governments or just plain do-gooders. To make things still worse, there

is no single factor or combination of factors in a situation that will necessarily trigger development if properly incited.[1]

It is in consequence of these several considerations that one faces the
problem of control over development.

On identifying the development urge

With development thus comprehensive, with the application of knowledge or insight into it thus interactive, and with the role of people or
agencies thus intersubjective, could it still be possible to tell head from
tail? Can one still envisage some specific entity, functioning in respect
to a development situation, whose signal feature it would be to be the
initiator or instigator (or, for that matter, helmsman or brakeman) for
another, probably larger, entity constituting the development situation?
In plain English, can one still think of some sort of development agent
or change agent servicing a developing society?

This question offers an occasion to elaborate somewhat on the concept of "instance of development" that was introduced previously. For
the sake of analysis of a given development process, one could perhaps
try to distinguish between two interacting phenomena, namely a developing entity and within it that which signals the development impulse,
the effective moment. Terminologically, the two could be distinguished
as frame of development and instance of development. Against the
background of this distinction one could, for example, proceed to re-
define the entrepreneurship-innovation concept, in order to indicate the
function of effectuating a particular shift in the existing state of affairs:
one out of several that are implied in that state of affairs as its inherent
potentialities. In this manner it should be possible to conceptualize
action that is at once initiation and interaction. Its usual name, in
sociology, is emergence.[2]

On emergence and cumulative result

Attractive as this sounds, there remains an element of oversimplification

---

[1] The weak point in the often tacit premisses of quite a few innovation and
entrepreneurship studies intended to be relevant to development. Comp. Everett
E. Hagen, *On the Theory of Social Change, How Economic Growth Begins*
(Homewood, Ill., Dorsey, 1962); David C. McClelland, *The Achieving Society*
(Princeton, N.J., Van Nostrand, 1961).

[2] Curiously, the term does not immediately come to mind in the connection.
This is because the term action, in its usual common speech sense, seems quite
different. In order to see that the term emergence applies one must remember
that we are here using the term action in a more abstract sense than activity of
an agent.

in it that must be taken care of before it could be considered workable. The point is that the grammatical singular used in the term "instance of development" may prove misleading. In actual fact, the word instance is used here in the categorical, not necessarily singular mode. Most likely, if there is one emergent urge or tendency it will be the resultant of the interaction – whether competitive or cumulative or both – between plural impulses. These would more or less simultaneously bring to the surface diverse inherent potentialities of a given situation, in response to roughly the same overall conditions and events, yet perhaps pinpointed in again diverse ways.[3] One and the same problematic state

[3] The proposition concerning the emergence of trends etc. inherent in a given situation as its potentialities, raises a fundamental question. It cannot receive adequate treatment within the present frame; but it should at least be mentioned. Phrased succinctly, it refers to the nature of this kind of emergence: whether it is random or not. In other words, do there, or do there not, exist contextual factors that will, in however complicated a fashion, exert a determining impact? Are there probabilities that emergence will occur in regard to particular "points" within an entire situation?

This matter has various sides. One of these, the question of retrospective versus prospective insight, will come up for consideration elsewhere in this essay. Another one, different but not quite separate, has been discussed recently in a somewhat different connection, namely of evolutionary theory as approached in terms of mathematics. (Comp. a review by J. L. Harper in *Science*, Vol. 160, No. 3826, 26 Apr. 1968, p. 408, of P. S. Moorhead and N. M. Kaplan (eds.), *Mathematical Challenges to the Neo-Darwinian Interpretation of Evolution, A Symposium*, Philadelphia, Wistar Institute, 1967.)

Upon purely aprioristic consideration of the matter, two schools of thought appear possible. The one would opt for sheer randomness as a matter of principle. The other would be more deterministic, in a rather special sense of the word. Starting out from the assumption that societal process operates, amongst other things, in terms of meaningful relationships, and assuming furthermore that even though the innumerable relationships involved need not add up to one consistent, let alone homogenous, complex or pattern, it would yet anticipate certain implications of these assumed characteristics of reality for the relative probability of particular emergences: in short it would stand for a degree of non-randomness.

Undoubtedly this option has immediate significance for the problem, to be discussed below, of consistency in development plans versus relative inconsistency in development situations. Those who would hold on to the former option are bound to face there a full-scale dilemma, namely between necessary consistency on the one hand and fundamental inconsistency and randomness on the other. This would entail a tremendous burden placed squarely on the *liberum arbitrium* of man the planner. This viewpoint loses much of the attraction it might have for some as soon as one realizes that its logical implication is complete detachment of man from context: an idea that was acceptable enough in the 19th century Western countries but that has lost most of its glory by now.

According to the latter option, for an apparently more deterministic viewpoint, one faces less of a dilemma. Rather, it is a kind of gap between relatively minimal consistency in development situation as against optimal consistency in

of affairs may be conceived as a slum problem by some, as a problem of race discrimination by others, as a poverty problem by others again, and so forth. Accordingly, the responses offered are likely to show diverse urges. If and to the extent to which their diversity would diminish, they could be expected to gather more developmental momentum. This brings to mind the seldom expressed realization that underdevelopment is in a way a condition where the possibilities, whether social, economic, political or even cultural, are inadequately explored and their realization neglected. It is disconcerting to see how in many cases even the resources and resourcefulness that could be harnessed for purposes of national liberation were in most cases no longer available once independence had been achieved.

The matter of various ways of pinpointing ties in with another, quite important problem: indicators of development. This will be taken up separately, as the argument proceeds.

Agent and context: a matter of ad hoc operational distinction

Returning now to the distinction between developing entity and development impulse. Arguing further along this line, one may draw consequences leading in two different directions. On the one hand, they refer to the "internal" functioning of a sociocultural entity that is developing; on the other hand, they refer to what occurs between various developing entities.

---

development plan. This could seem to leave less scope for man's discretion; but it raises accordingly less doubt concerning the relevance of human action in respect of the human context, sociocultural reality as instanced in a given situation.

Of the two options, the latter would seem preferable. The main reason lies in the already mentioned meaningful character of relationships (or in more exact phrasing: of operational relationships between *ad hoc* sociocultural entities). This is the point that will be normally defended by saying that in one's intellectual dealings with societal phenomena one must bear in mind that in the last resort one deals with man. (Note, besides, that the old argument concerning the rationality inherent in reality cannot validly enter here.) Now in consequence of this preference, one faces the question of how to go about studying the factors determining the occurrence of particular convergences in a given development situation. In the present connection, this issue can only be raised, not effectively tackled. However, it would appear that further study of development, as a variant of societal process, would depend upon the conceptualization and subsequent identification of clusters of operational relationships that, in interacting, determine the specificity of a given situation. Given these, the study could refer mainly to the modalities of interaction both within and between such clusters.

In the former respect, one can envisage an important and useful distinction between two operational levels. One would be the level of the total entity going through development, as constituted by its plural components: whether live persons, social groups or whatever. The other would be the level at which some particular component(s) [4] would function as the moment of manifestation/effectuation of a shift in the prevailing state of affairs: the emergent developmental impulse. This distinction is crucial, theoretically as well as practically. You can be an agent of development whilst being one out of the collectivity going through that development, but you ruin your chances in the former respect when confounding your member role with your role as agent. In fact, you must take considerable care to make the one correspond to the other, not merely so far as you are concerned but particularly so far as the others are.

Rephrasing this in more theoretical terms, there is no room for the Promethean role that has tended to loom so large in the self-view of many a development officer or planning agency. But this does not mean that they have no role to fulfil. To that role, the one crucial consideration is that either you get across to people or you will be stuck high and dry with your preconceived ideas. The only characteristic that will effectively distinguish between development policy and colonial rule (or its equivalent, charitative condescension) is the systematic effort to "get across". This point has come up previously under a different name (because it was considered from the opposite viewpoint), namely as participation.

Another way of elucidating this matter is to say that the entity that functions as change agent is not an invariant but, much to the contrary, a covariant. It is bound to undergo change whilst being effective as a change agent. It could be argued that one of the major reasons why transfer of sovereignty became the way out of trouble in cases like Indonesia and Algeria is precisely that the colonizers were the legitimate agents, not to say monopolists, of change, and that, moreover, they assumed themselves to be invariants. This applies most dramatically to the Eurasians of Indonesia and the *colons* of Algeria, but it applies as well to the Dutch and the metropolitan French. And is it too far-fetched to

---

[4] Regardless whether a permanent component or an *ad hoc* one. In the foregoing, I spoke on purpose of an entity functioning in respect to a development situation. There and here, the intention is to obliterate any difference between inside and outside agents. Too many promising studies have been marred by the unwarranted introduction of this distinction.

see some not too distant parallels in the contemporary U.S. scene? [5]

In respect of what occurs between several entities each in its own way subject to development, much the same obtains in principle. With

[5] This is perhaps the occasion to venture some further remarks on the change agent, who has already been under fire more than once in the preceding. As argued, the subject-object dichotomy between agent on the one hand and society, community or group on the other, must be rejected. In the same manner certain other distinctions, often applied in the connection, are not acceptable without qualification. They run between (1) internal and external agent, (2) self-purposive and altruistic agent, (3) agent who simply applies prescriptive knowledge and he who cannot simply apply pre-existent know-how and must seek instead for viable goals and means of action. As regards the first and second distinctions, they are at best secondary, given the overriding importance of considerations in regard to the matter of relevance of what the agent stands for, does or is, in his operational context. If what he does or is is indeed relevant, the question whether he is an insider or an outsider need not be decisive for his success. Nor are his motivations likely to be subject to prior scrutiny. But if not, there is little chance that his being an insider or his altruism will save the day for him. As to the third distinction, its importance tends to be overrated. The difference in position between a public health officer and a community development worker is not nearly so clear and fundamental as it may appear at first sight. It might be, if the former had a firm basis in a set of clear and unchangeable notions about health and disease, accepted both by himself and those whom he is to serve. There is no reason to believe that this is usually the case. In fact, even in the West these notions have tended most of the time to be subject to considerable change.

From change agent to expert is but one step. A small step, indeed, inasmuch as expert knowledge is quite often made to serve as the rationalization why a change agent is needed at all and furthermore why a certain person or kind of persons should be selected for the job. In many cases, the terms expert and change agent are virtually synonymous. In many other cases, the two are twinned so as to perform one job. In any case, the expert status is subject to all the doubts and restrictions that follow from considerations of relevance. At the same time, the expert himself usually works under conditions where he can hardly afford to be bothered by such doubts. With all due respect for genuine competence and indubitable sincerity, one cannot help from time to time to feel quite concerned about what experts are and do (and also, surely, about the role one has to play and the things one has to do any time one is cast in the expert's role). The constant recourse to so-called generalities, the undisturbed equanimity, the ever benevolent manner in which the final verdict is given in invariably prescriptive manner, they are each and everyone necessary assets that the expert brings to his work. They are his defence mechanism against inevitable disappointments and against the risks of becoming monopolized by one party in some locally prevailing strife that is irrelevant to the matter that necessitates his presence. At the same time, however, they risk to become his armour against effective involvement and real commitment, even against struggling for actual relevance of that which he knows and does to the context in which he works. A collective work like Richard J. Ward (ed.), *The Challenge of Development, Theory and Practice* (Chicago, Aldine, 1967), in which ever so many experts are lined up, each giving in almost irresponsibly brief compass his expert vision of one segment of development action, is not merely disappointing but in fact disquieting for precisely these reasons.

an eye to current practice, it deserves more emphasis, however. The reason is that the usually added element of cross-cultural operations is indeed a formidable complication, and one that needs carefully to be accounted for. We did not really need *The Ugly American* [6] to become aware of this fact. On the other hand, we do not really know, even today, how to do the accounting job involved.

[6]   William J. Lederer and Eugene Burdick, *The Ugly American* (London, Gollancz, 1959).

PART III

ON GOAL SETTING AND FEED-BACK:
THE MATTER OF EVALUATION

8

INTRODUCTION: GOALS AS CRITERIA

There is yet a fifth major question in regard to development that attracts
an increasing amount of attention. Currently it tends to go by the name
of evaluation. Development agencies all over the world begin to show
an increasing concern about the actual results of their work, as compared to hoped-for results. But inasmuch as many, if not all, of these
agencies are under the necessity to vindicate their existence, they are
not too well placed for the purpose. And they know it.

Evaluation: recognized need and inevitable aversion

Consequently what they tend to come up with, most of the times when
they make the attempt, is either rosy apologetics (nicely matched, now
and then, by the alarmist criticisms of their detractors), or more or less
prescriptive, quite general statements on how one might undertake some
evaluative studies. This is clearly a matter of having either to overshoot
the mark or to fall short of it. It is not difficult to name some of the
factors that make this so.

For one thing, it is extremely hard, for most of those concerned, to
accept that development processes, and consequently also development
action, are quite wasteful. Some closer consideration of development as
a variant of process should confirm beyond doubt that this is in the
natural order of things. But with taxpayers' or investors' moneys involved it is somewhat awkward to say these things aloud. They are
unlikely to be understood, let alone accepted.

Another factor involved, and a most unfortunate one at a first
glance, is the terrible mix-up between Cold War strategy and development assistance or, as it is called nowadays, international cooperation.
This matter will be taken up below.

Having thus cleared away some underbrush, we can proceed to tackle
the matter in its broader perspective.

The natural limits of general theory

There would seem to be little prospect for evaluation theories or techniques that would run in strictly general terms and that would employ one set, however broad, of formal criteria. Too much of the selfhood, the exclusive specificity of the sociocultural entities concerned is too critically at stake in development. These demand to be accounted for in the first place. It is only with them as given frames of reference, that it could make sense to speak of sets, that is, more or less consistent pluralities, of criteria.

This is not meant to imply that *a priori* general theorizing is anathema. Rather it repeats and underscores what everybody knows but most of us find hard to do whenever we remember to try it, namely that the formal elements of general theory need to be reconsidered, and perhaps rephrased and recomposed, in order that their relevance to a given real situation be effectively established. It is hardly necessary to recall here how much generality of social sciences theory and techniques is in fact Western generality, and with what astounding ease both Westerners and Western-trained non-Westerners tend to expand their application (but not their applicability) to clearly non-Western situations. Nor is it necessary to point out that the term non-Western is a blatant misnomer for any purposes: what it hides, whilst supposed to sum it up, is a large number of highly diverse sociocultural entities existing under quite various circumstances.

One central question is therefore how to develop evaluation theory, and how to improve and develop current evaluation techniques, so as to warrant the expectation that their application to a given development situation could make sense. Crucial to this purpose is the matter of development goals even prior to that of measurable indicators of development.

The crucial importance of goals

As a rule, development experts and agencies, including governments of developing countries, will be inclined to envisage development goals in a manner that derives from standard preconceived notions rather than from fresh observation of actual, and as a rule quite bewildering, reality. Reality, if it enters the scene at all, will have to come as feed-back upon the implementation of policies devised in accordance with those notions. This is not because the people concerned are fools but rather because they are only human. The point is that they are up against a formidable difficulty. The difficulty, namely, of identifying the goals that obtain in a given situation, and the pattern, quite changeable as a rule, in which these goals are interrelated. There are, as yet, rarely any effective procedures for identifying goals and their patterns. In their absence, systems devised to serve as frames of reference, whether for development policies or for development evaluation, are doomed to remain to a large extent aprioristic and to suffer from unchecked ethnocentrism: they are not really general, and of doubtful relevance. Can we expect any improvement of conditions in this regard?

Goals are necessarily specific

From what was said above on process and modalities of development, it would seem to follow that goals in any development situation are bound to be specific to that situation. The point was already made. In fact, the goals are nothing but a second, more articulated and perhaps more institutionalized, stage in the manifestation of a novel direction or convergence in an ongoing state of affairs. Goals are a manifest but provisional crystallization, potentially with a voluntaristic moment, of what we have previously called the selective urge towards implementation of certain potentialities inherent in a given state of affairs, a given sociocultural entity. (The urge, as such, occurring usually in response to that state of affairs proving problematic in certain respects.)

Thus considered, the term goals will refer to a conceptual category, in the framework of development process, much more general than it is usually taken to be. At the same time, actual goals remain to be identified in the given situation. We have returned, clearly, to the question how to identify them. But hopefully we are somewhat better placed now to make the effort.

9

ON THE IDENTIFICATION OF GOALS

A double procedure for identification

There are clearly two kinds of procedures that apply to the identification of goals in given development situations. One is by and large inductive, the other could be called deductive. One works by means of clues available in the concrete situation with which one happens to be concerned; the other centres around the attempt to apply to such a situation the elements of pre-existent theory of a supposedly general nature. The former, being apparently the more difficult of the two, tends to receive less attention than the latter. This is not necessarily correct. The two should somehow be balanced. This however, could hardly be easy, less so since it is by no means clear how they could be harmonized, as a prerequisite to being kept in balance for purposes of goal identification.

Inductive procedures

As regards the former, it is useful to introduce a further distinction. It runs between emergent tendencies on the one hand and effective residues on the other.

By emergent tendencies is meant the concurrence of a dissatisfaction, disaffection or need with a novel urge in response thereto. It is more or less the same as what some writers call turning points. It is the emergent focussing or convergence of our previous discussion on development as a variant of process.

By effective residues is meant something close to, but not fully the same as, Pareto's residues. One element of the definition of change and development that was given above is selectiveness. As argued above, a change moment or development moment can be conceived that will feature as a limited occurrence within a necessarily wider context. It is entirely possible within the framework of this approach to pick out for consideration, in a given situation, not those component elements that feature as the change moment or development moment but on the contrary those that are not immediately part of change/development and that, on account of being not immediately affected or involved, feature as relatively stable. (It is to them that such concepts as cultural lag would apply.) When turning to those, one is bound to realize that the fact that they are not immediately affected says nothing about their importance or effectiveness as component elements of the situation concerned. More precisely, it is entirely possible that as components of that situation they remain fully effective determinants, in their own right, of comprehensive processes going on. There are various customary expressions for this realization. One of them says that no innovation has a chance that does not somehow fit in the context in which it occurs or into which it is introduced. Simple and obvious as such a statement sounds, it has a rather broader and more profound significance than is usually attributed to it.

Note once again that the relationship between emergent tendencies and effective residues in a given situation is a matter of interest in itself. Whatever may result from change and whatever development will occur, will to a considerable extent follow from the "give and take" between these two kinds of determinants.

Schematic elaboration

In schematic presentation, the preceding enumeration appears on the next page.

With the help of this chart some further elucidation may be achieved. The left and middle columns repeat schematically what has just been stated above. The column on the right hand side shows how, starting from the distinction between three sources of clues, a range of clues can be set up that does not show very crude breaks either between effective residues and emergent tendencies or even between inductive and deductive procedures.

Classification of clues toward identification of development goals

Thus the category of felt needs or manifest tendencies would be typically determined by effective residues as well as by emergent tendencies. A good example is the urge towards national independence (and more broadly, towards national self-realization). If one were to distinguish in its regard between effective residues and emergent tendencies, one would have to break it down into components, some of which could be ranged under the one heading and some under the other.

Again, there are cases in which clues inductively established come near to merging with those deductively established. The urge to do away with poverty is almost, but not quite, the same as the economist's adhortation to increase per capita income. The two do not fully coincide on account of difference in implications on either side. The urge to do away with poverty refers to poverty as perceived by those concerned and the economist's adhortation will consciously or unconsciously re-

Elements towards identification of goals in specific instances of development process

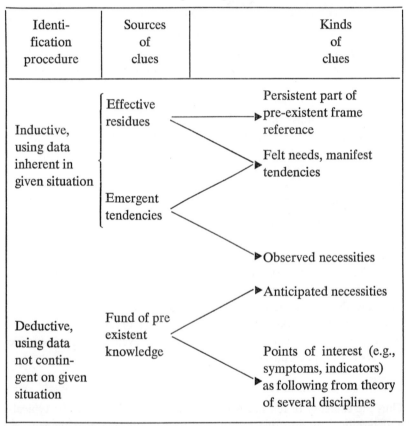

Identi- fication procedure	Sources of clues	Kinds of clues
Inductive, using data inherent in given situation	Effective residues Emergent tendencies	Persistent part of pre-existent frame reference Felt needs, manifest tendencies Observed necessities
Deductive, using data not contin-gent on given situation	Fund of pre existent knowledge	Anticipated necessities Points of interest (e.g., symptoms, indicators) as following from theory of several disciplines

flect norms that probably derive from elsewhere. Recall that the gulf of difference between the U.S. antipoverty campaign and the redistribution of national income in certain European welfare states derives from a comparable kind of discrepancy in ultimate orientations. Much the same goes for the urge to do away with disease as compared with the public health officer's activities. Even in regard to the urge to do away with ignorance – to complete the *trias* – one must beware of the too easy assumption that those desirous to acquire knowledge and those desirous to disseminate it refer to really the same thing and have really the same goals in mind.

Even so, that which features in the chart as observed necessities and that which features as anticipated necessities are close together. In fact, the closer together, the better: a curious element enters here, namely the desirability that the gap between the two procedures for finding clues be bridged as much as possible.

Inductive and deductive procedures must complement one another

This introduces a further point emerging from the scheme. In many cases the gap is not bridged or insufficiently so. The deductive procedure tends to be predominant, which is perhaps in keeping with the lack in symmetry between developed and underdeveloped parts of the world in the matter of taking initiatives towards development action. For too many purposes and on too many occasions, the identification of development goals proceeds on an exclusively or almost exclusively deductive basis. It cannot be repeated often enough that here lies one of the fundamental weaknesses of much development action, and one of the main causes of frustration.

Towards further elaboration of the scheme

The next move along the line of argument followed hitherto should be, first, to spell out in further detail the five headings in the right hand column of the scheme and, secondly, to provide insight into the question how the many items that would undoubtedly have to be listed under each of these five headings will add up so as to constitute one set of clues towards the identification of development goals in a given situation. No doubt, in either move it will be necessary to refer to one specific development situation: the entire operation is repeatable *ad infinitum*, so long as one runs into development situations not yet dealt with.

Now these are considerations that raise one very practical question. How much of all this should, or for that matter could, find a place within the present essay?

As regards the deductive part, much has been done by others that needs neither repeating nor even summarizing here. In particular economists and more recently also political scientists are effective producers of insight into what are crucial matters for purposes both of development policy making and analysis of development: "points of interest", as the scheme calls them. Indeed theory in these fields is quite geared, and increasingly equipped, to point out, in essentially aprioristic fashion and in strictly general (that is, timeless and placeless) terms, which phenomena are important for the purpose of identifying development goals.

In regard to the matter of what the scheme calls "anticipated needs", conditions are perhaps somewhat less satisfactory. It may therefore be interesting to undertake some exercise (ch. 10) concerning that side of things, even if this will have to be done in summary fashion given the present scope. It is proposed to restrict this exercise to one discipline, namely sociology. This restriction follows naturally from the writer's limitations, not from any fundamental preference. It is, moreover, resorted to with some misgivings, because it might give the impression that a unidisciplinary approach is here advocated as valid and effective. Such an impression would be wrong. According to the reasoning followed in this essay, the unidisciplinary approach in a matter like this is little more than a first preparation for an effectively interdisciplinary, comprehensive approach; and from the former to the latter is more than a simple step. Even so, one must start from the beginning, and this is what will be attempted.

As regards the inductive part, rather less has been done, certainly in proportion to the number of development situations that demand attention. It seems therefore appropriate to take some exercise in this regard again. This time, the writer's limitations indicate a strong preference for the Middle East as one broad development situation. In choosing an entire culture area, the notion of development situation is clearly taken in its broadest sense. Within it, a number of (sub-)situations could be distinguished, each of which could be selected for more detailed study along the lines to be followed here. In taking this exercise, an attempt will be made to differentiate between the three kinds of clues distinguished in the scheme: chapters 11, 12 and 13 respectively.

10

ANTICIPATED NECESSITIES: THE SOCIOLOGICAL VIEW

The matter of "anticipated necessities" according to the sociologist's view will be discussed here with two basic considerations in mind. One is that a viable way to anticipate development needs is to differentiate between a broad profile of a "developed" situation and the same of an underdevelopment situation. What matters for the purpose are the signal differences emerging from comparison of the two. The other basic consideration is purposeful restriction to the sociological view-point. This means that in two ways the present discussion remains incomplete. First, it will be left to the economist, political scientist, social psychologist and whatever further social scientists should play a role in the connection, to deal each in his own way with his own aspect of sociocultural reality. A full presentation of the matter would no doubt require contributions from all sides. Secondly, no attempt will be made to broach the vital problem of the ultimate integration of all these aspect-wise approaches into one consistent pattern of intellectual dealings with reality. No more can be offered here than what the Germans would call a *Probe*, a limited exercise meant to demonstrate what is involved in the procedure here advocated. The exercise will be limited also in the sense that a limited number of points will be selected for discussion: enough to warrant the hope that on this basis the matter could be further pursued by others and on other occasions.[1]

(1) SECULARIZATION AND SEGMENTATION

In a situation of underdevelopment, secularizing tendencies are likely to appear as acute and pernicious, whereas in a developed situation, they

---

[1] The following sections represent a thoroughly revised version of a paper first published in Dutch, in *Mens en Maatschappij*, 36 (Amsterdam, 1961), and summarized in English in my *Cross-Cultural Studies* (The Hague, Mouton, 1963). The present revision was made on the basis of an English translation of the original made by Mrs. J. Sanders.

are somehow more endemic and perennial without endangering survival.

This fact is of greater importance than is usually recognized. There-fore, besides being given pride of place, it will also be discussed in somewhat more detail than the points that will follow.

Theocentric and secular urges: a complementarity to the West

The God postulated in the Christian faith is, with a variation on Rudolf Otto's [2] term, *der ganz Andere*. He is The Absolute, in the sense that, notwithstanding the existential relationship between them (indicated in such complexes as revelation and faith), the concepts "God" and "man" can under no circumstances reciprocally define each other. Man is creature. Consequently, Christian doctrine is an absolute command-ment: "love thy neighbour as thyself", etc. The absoluteness of this doctrine also shows its essential impracticability. This basic datum of the human condition is accounted for (rather than asserted) in Christian dogma, namely in a repudiating, deprecating sense. A signal expression is the tenet concerning original sin. It appears again in the sociocultural practice of Christianity. Along with Christian doctrine, and dialectically inherent in it, an element of inevitable non-Christianity occurs as a basic datum: a fundamental secularization trend. Accordingly, to Chris-tian perception, the circumstance that Western civilization is doubly rooted (namely in Christianity and in humanism) is not a mere coinci-dence. It is necessarily so: it demonstrates the fundamental human condition. In this view, the secularization trend is not merely accounted for, it is allotted its proper place. It is an essentially secondary, even though utterly inevitable, deviation occurring side by side with the Christian pattern. Although thus impugned, this pattern stands un-impaired: it is presupposed. Therefore, secularization, that is: everything in life that "aims away from God", much as it constitutes the denial of Christianity, cannot really affect it. Whilst necessarily coexistent with "fundamental Christianity", to borrow S. Angus's [3] term, it cannot obliterate it. This is a matter of cardinal importance for the under-standing of the "developed" situation, because it occurs in a culture context determined by the state of affairs just discussed. More so, since it loses little of its significance in a so-called post-Christian era, in which Western civilization is supposed to be now.

[2]   Rudolf Otto, *Das Heilige* (München, Beck, 1936).
[3]   S. Angus, *Essential Christianity* (London, Murray, 1939).

The segmentation of Western sociocultural reality

With secularization thus contradictory to, yet inherent in, established religion, the conditions are given for a sociocultural phenomenon that deserves especially to be noted here. It is the phenomenon of the segmentation or parcellation of life. Given the inevitability of secularization tendencies, religion is bound to appear as something by itself, an entity in its own right. Consequently, it can be perceived as distinct from the fullness of life, from the comprehensiveness of sociocultural reality. This possibility of distinction, once realized, is bound to open up a range of similar possibilities to distinguish particular aspects or segments from the fullness of existence. Next to "the religious", other aspects of life may become distinct, as, *e.g.*, "the political" or "the economic". Once distinguished, they may be objectified and even institutionalized. This surely is how the "social system" comes by its "sub-systems". (And that it is not necessarily an easy process to go through is convincingly demonstrated by the strife that has for ages obtained between church and state in Europe.) But – and this is not always remembered – it is not any and every social system that does more or less necessarily get equipped, in this manner, with sub-systems of this particular kind.

By contrast: comprehensive religiosity

In a society whose religious basis is formed by the monolithic religiosity particularly characteristic of some non-Christian religions, like Islam or – *bien étonnés de se trouver ensemble* – Hinduism, the situation is bound to be different. The difference will vary in its turn, according to which non-Christian religion one chooses in order to argue the point. By way of illustration for present purposes, some remarks may find a place here that refer mainly to the Middle East and the Indian subcontinent plus their offshoots such as Indonesia. It is quite immaterial whether the religion concerned is Islam or Hinduism, or some "primitive" paganism, or a mystical philosophy such as Buddhism, or even some pseudo-orthodoxy like "Marxism-Leninism".[4] A follower of such a religion, together with the entire society of which he is part, lives in a universe that is totally permeated by religiously phrased basic notions. In principle, these have no latitude whatsoever for secularization trends, that is to say, for tendencies towards a conduct of life irrespective of the religious basis. Undoubtedly, they differentiate between sacral and profane, but this is something else than the difference between the orienta-

---

[4] J. Grenier, *Essai sur l'esprit de l'orthodoxie* (Paris, Gallimard, 1938).

tion "towards God" and the tendency towards secularization that appears in Christian thought. Potentially, the profane is fully implied in the sacral and, in principle, the one can absorb the other any time. On the other hand, the secularization tendency inherent in Christianity is the exponent of a fundamentally different manner of thought and life than the one that engenders the differentiation between sacral and profane. Consequently, secularization in this specific sense is something alien to a sociocultural universe based on the monolithic religious principle: the preconditions for its occurrence are simply not there.

Secularization verus corrosion of religiosity

Now the matter would still be fairly easy and comprehensible if all this would mean that one could say: no secularization, in our sense of the word, in culture areas determined by monolithic religiosity. The point is that this conclusion is neither true nor false, but true to an extent. Indeed there is much in the culture areas concerned that goes by the name of secularization, but that is in fact nothing worse than laxity. Relatively few Muslims observe all their religious duties; in fact, those who do tend to be fairly conspicuous. This, however, will hardly be producive of conditions such as a crisis of conscience, whether acute or more or less permanent. And an appeal to the lax Muslim's identification as a Muslim will be at least as effective as the same appeal addressed to the zealous Muslim.

On the other hand, there are cases of secularization, in the special sense in which it is used here, occurring in the culture contexts under consideration. Cases, in other words, where men find themselves torn between active or passive conforming to the religiously permeated, monolithic universe in which they have been brought up and the agony of desire to break the indépassabilité of that universe, for example by throwing out allegiance to its religious component – which, at this very occasion, is for the first time distinguished as such. Whenever such phenomena occur, there is cause for two conclusions that are part of one and the same diagnosis. First, the universe concerned has perished; it has broken into fragments. Some of these fragments may eventually become reinstated as (parts of) a new order, others may not. Secondly, the society in question is actually struggling for survival; the very grounds for its existence as a sociocultural entity are at stake.

Underdevelopment, cross-cultural complications, secularization

The point in this long digression is that the religiously inspired mono-lithic pattern is pre-eminent in many of the areas that are currently de-scribed as underdeveloped. Quite often it is decidedly non-Christian, as in the examples given above; but there is no reason to believe that it could never bear the hallmark of an older non-Western variety of Christianity. Now this can only mean that in many cases underdevelop-ment must be considered in the light of the preceding analysis.

The present period is one in which many societies experience the urge towards renewed sociocultural self-perception and self-assertion. This drive for new or renewed self-realization will necessarily refer back to the inherited religious basic pattern. This applies in a particularly dramatic way whenever the expectation of freedom is involved, with its inevitable millennial or even eschatological connotations. So far, there are no difficulties. But given the historical context in which the urge to-wards new sociocultural self-realization occurs, complications are bound to arise that tend to produce the kind of secularization phenomena just alluded to. The point is that it is inevitable that the traditional, mono-lithic religious basis is not the only determinant of the tendencies charac-teristic of underdevelopment.

Other determinants, totally unrelated to this religious basis, play an equally important role; and the very fact that they are placed in juxta-position to the latter unavoidably makes them feature, regardless of what-ever they may signify in other connections, as secularization tendencies.

Obviously, the major cause of these complications is the circumstance that underdevelopment occurs in the perspective of development else-where: that is, in some effective relationship with alien culture areas and thus with basically alien ideas and orientations. A good many of the guiding principles that appear as tendencies in underdevelopment situations originate in what people have observed, or thought they ob-served, in, or as coming from, the developed regions. Applied to their own situation, these are necessarily disruptive: not being part of the consistent monolithic pattern of thought and action that represents the traditional order. Note that this consideration applies regardless of whether the newly introduced element be spiritual or material, religious or technological, and equally regardless of whether, in the developed region from where it derives, it belongs to the sector described above as being oriented towards a divine sense of purpose or rather to that of the secularizing tendencies.

Underdevelopment as secularization

The alien element is at once a secularizing tendency in the rather special sense in which the term is used here, and an agent of the segmentation that was hitherto unknown (the universe being "monolithic") and that, in culture contexts determined by the Western variants of Christianity, follows from its inherent element of secularization. Note furthermore that, whether factor of segmentation (not necessarily segmentation along Western lines!) or secularizing tendency, it is bound to be virulent and perhaps pernicious. After all, the mere fact that this tendency occurs challenges, and lays bare for the first time, the basic principles of the order with which it is meant to coexist henceforth. Fundamentally speaking, it renders the very existence of such an order impossible. Indeed, as was said above, the period of acute underdevelopment is in fact a period of sociocultural, including religious, crisis for the societies concerned.

The crisis of segmentation

Such a crisis may prove explosive. If so, the international press will appear on the scene like a pack of vultures, fulfilling its great mission to give everyone in the world his fair share of the sensation; and worsening things by doing so.

Fortunately, the explosive cases are less numerous than those in which the accumulated flammable material continues to smoulder, often under an apparently harmless surface. The crisis may either go entirely unrecognized, or alternatively it may be recognized to a limited extent, thus losing its real significance. Sometimes this blurring results from the dexterity with which those in control manipulate an as yet inadequately effective public opinion; more often it may be inherent in the thought models that happen to be employed to further the urge towards new sociocultural self-realization. Thus, for example, the very process of political liberation, particularly if it follows after a period of resistance with its unifying effect. Thus, for another example, the idealized prospect of material betterment to be achieved through temporary sacrifice. It is typical of a smouldering crisis of this sort that almost everyone, for reasons unclear even to himself, will feel discontent and at the same time something that could almost be called a chronically bad conscience. No circumstances could be more propitious to the conscious or unconsious exploitation of modern techniques of massification and to the subsequent domination of the masses. It is a state of affairs which threatens to pervert the prevailing disorientation, of both individuals and society, into the pseudo-orientation of some overheated orthodoxy and thereby to conceal it. This sort of orthodoxy, curiously, will often have to belie its basic religious impetus equally much as its inherent threat of secularization: and this regardless whether it is known as nationalism, anti-imperialism, anti-colonialism, development ideology, or a combination of all these and perhaps others. The reason is that it cannot validly and effectively tie in with, and pretend to continue, the kind of religiosity permeating the inherited monolithic sociocultural pattern, nor can it afford (whether in terms of self-identification or for purposes of acceptability to its followers) to stand for the secularization-disruption trend just analyzed.

The urge to reunify

In a way, therefore, the emergent *ad hoc* orthodoxy and the post-independence malaise are one and the same thing. They mark the moment when people realize that if things are perhaps not what they might be, this may be due to other than incidental and external causes. Underdevelopment is an inherited state of affairs, combined with a novel consciousness in its regard on the part of those who constitute it. Using an awkward metaphor: those concerned realize suddenly that until "the moment of underdevelopment", sociocultural energies available were (by the standards obtaining henceforth) frittered away rather than cumulative; their effectiveness was fundamentally limited, and they were hardly geared to distinct and consistent purposes. At a given moment, all this is recognized as underdevelopment, and the crucial question ensuing from this recognition refers to channeling these energies, providing them with direction. From subsistence to maximization of effort.

Here the argument has run full circle and returns to the *ad hoc* orthodoxy. The main conditioning factor for the emergence of these *ad hoc* quasi-orthodoxies is their singular usefulness as instruments to channel and direct sociocultural energies that are available in more or less latent form. They are a prerequisite, if not the sufficient condition, for development.

Curiously, the *ad hoc* orthodoxy that succeeds – and to an extent was perhaps already present in – the liberation movement implies drastic restrictions of a freedom that has barely been attained. In a way, this proves no more than that independence is not freedom, and that the freedom that independence brings could prove to be no more, fundamentally, than chaos. More important, it is instrumental in differentiating between freedoms, and towards ascertaining the viability limits of each.

Parallel hereto, the inherited and fixed pattern of needs, material and other, has become loose; and nothing could prevent needs from proving limitless and, much more important, unforeseeable because unknown, except a conscious move away from unsatisfaction to limited and discerning satisfaction. The allocation of priorities is much more than a pedestrian affair needed for sorry reasons: it is the conscious attempt to build a cosmos in which the ongoing effort towards betterment is implied as one of its crucial elements.

Development and religious disintegration

To round off this section, the question must be raised when the development effort, through *ad hoc* orthodoxy (for example, single party system) or otherwise, leaves religion as an all-permeating but non-isolable element of the monolithic sociocultural patterns here under review. Recall how, according to the present view, the so-called developed countries of the "Christian" West have converted the fundamental conflict between God-oriented and other-oriented thought and action (which emerged at a particular stage of their history) into a source of sociocultural energy by providing that energy with a direction, a purpose.

Regardless now of that purpose, which is extremely hard to define or summarize (a quite significant fact in itself!), one notes how in certain so-called underdeveloped areas, of monolithic, religiously inspired cultural tradition, secularization, not merely the "laxity" variant, but also and in particular the fundamental "disruption" variant, appears as an acute problem. This happens precisely at the time when (and maybe because) to the people concerned the inherited state of affairs becomes a matter of purposive concern. Survival (and with it the success of the urge towards renewed self-realization of the sociocultural entities concerned) depends on whether it will prove possible to deal successfully, that is creatively, with the secularization-disruption problem.

Now, if at some points there may be some parallelism with the Western situation, it ends here. The West was able to (and had to) deal with the matter within the scope of its very religious pattern of thought and action. The areas now under consideration are unable to do so and must come to terms with it rather within the scope of the secularizing trend, beyond the pale of religion proper (conceived, falsely, as a distinct segment of life). This greatly aggravates the difficulty, and it is likely that some very hard battles, on various grounds, may have to be fought before it becomes clear how one can try to come to terms with the problems. The Tunisian case provides some pointers in the connection, and something can be learned from the failures of certain Indian policy makers who thought they had the solution in their pockets.

Also the U.S.S.R. could be mentioned in the connection. Without delving now into the question what could be presented as the religiously inspired, monolithic, sociocultural pattern of Tsarist Russia, or into the question what exactly qualifies for labeling as the secularization tendency, the Russian revolution is a case of secularization *cum* disruption, the communist state that followed it a case of *ad hoc* orthodoxy, and development effort is the proper name for what has been going on ever since. There is an affinity between the U.S.S.R. and the developing countries that was only partly studied by E. Sarkisyanz [5] and that not merely eludes the West, but actually thwarts even their best intended efforts at development assistance.

(2) INCOHERENCE OF ORGANIZATIONAL TYPES

Underdevelopment is lack of variety in types of social organization. This point rephrases the disruption aspect of the argument in the previous section. The more or less monolithic appearance of inherited sociocultural patterns features now in its decay. Due to internal and external causes, it has ended up by appearing as unsatisfactory to those concerned. Not merely have traditional types of social organization been uprooted, some severely, others less so; new types have been adopted, but they have rarely struck root. The latter are usually of foreign origin, mostly Western. In being adapted to the new situation, they are often re-interpreted in such a manner as to become unrecognizable. Even so, they will not fit smoothly as components of an articulated society, *i.e.*, a society that is differentiated but nevertheless coherent and unified. On the contrary, they are like bricks that are carted to the building site long before a decision has been taken as to the type of building that is to be constructed.

This is not a drawback in itself since sociocultural structures cannot be built according to the *a priori* of a formal decree. It is only possible to determine *a posteriori* how some of the available building materials were discarded, some modified, and others apparently applied without alteration.

[5] Emanuel Sarkisyanz, *Russland und der Messianismus des Orients* (Tübingen, Mohr, 1955).

Similarity of social forms as lack of creativity

What does constitute a drawback, however, is the surprising uniformity, the conspicuous lack of diversity, shown by the types of social organization, old and new, which spring into prominence in an underdevelopment situation. The types of organization that arouse public interest all show a similar one-sidedness. On top of this, they preclude each other as a matter of principle.

The reason is that in order to be worth-while at all – this repeats to an extent what was said above on *ad hoc* orthodoxies – any new type of organization must be serviceable as a cumulation centre of sociocultural energy for the society in question, as a means whereby the available potential is gathered together and given a purpose. There can be no doubt about the purpose of gathering the forces in this way, nor about the continuities involved. What is first the effort to build power for the purpose of achieving independence must be launched once more in order to ensure the continued existence of the society under basically new conditions (independence, yet existence within view of the developed areas, also as part of the world as a whole). Any type of social organization that is created for this purpose cannot avoid virtually comprising – whilst remaking it – the society concerned as a whole. Consequently, no society can offer scope for more than one such organization form: this notwithstanding the fact that usually there are several candidates for the role. Thus emerge the dangers referred to above: essentially, they preclude each other, and actually they try to prevent each other from being positively effective in the manner each intended.

Inevitable uniformity of organizational types and politicization

It should be clear now that the uniformity of social organization forms is something inherent in and fundamental to underdevelopment situations. This consideration is further underscored by the circumstance that almost everyone of these organization "models" is expressed primarily in political terms. Certainly, the term "political" in this connection is bound to have a rather vague, partly foreign partly native tenor, of which formal and actual power continue to be the most conspicuous determinants.

The emergence of the political *per se* is normally one of the earlier symptoms of the disruption discussed above. A political expression that will produce the intended accumulation of all sociocultural energy, whether material or spiritual, is bound to appear primarily as a concentration of naked power,[6] and eventually also of its more sophisticated forms such as wealth, public opinion, or simply information. Such concentration of power, in its turn, identifies itself more easily by reference to that against which it is directed than to that which, in order to create it, it must perceive and, in order to perceive it, it must first create.

New organizational types inevitably provisional

Here one distinguishes yet another element of the uniformity discussed above: as sociocultural trends, the newly apparent types of social organization are purely *ad hoc*. The point was made above in regard to the one variant of these organization forms discussed there, the quasi-orthodoxy. As argued there, their relevance to the basic problems at stake may prove quite limited if not negative; they may cause the perennial significance of these issues to be hidden behind a smoke screen of utopian expectations that they arouse as a means to bolster the call for unity – "*seid einig, einig, einig*" – which in reality is often their only message. The purpose of the new unity is as yet undetermined, and threatens to remain undetermined. When this is the case, the entire movement or whatever it is risks to end up as fair game for some inner circle that is in control of all affairs, particularly the more profitable ones. Which is not all too different from pre-underdevelopment conditions.

Each organization type virtually comprehensive

Bearing all this in mind, it would seem characteristic of underdevelopment that the state, practically all parties, unions and associations, and numerous other traditional and newly introduced types of social organization, turn out to be of a more or less totalitaristic nature, either potentially or in fact. The driving urgency of the circumstances means that each and everyone of them is the potential embodiment of the entire society in question. In fact, it must appear to many of those concerned that under the circumstances no non-totalitaristic type of organization could be a valid proposition.

Available types of social organization mutually exclusive

Unfortunately, the uniformity is not limited to identical aims and tactics. As said above, all these types of organization are actually, and as a

---

[6] Frantz Fanon, *The Wretched of the Earth* (Harmondsworth, Penguin, 1967), marks this point clearly and dramatically in his argument about the crucial nature of violence.

matter of principle, mortal rivals of each other. Particularly the recipro-
cal exclusion signifies an effective impoverishment of sociocultural life,
or more precisely a premature and abortive turn in the trend that was
just setting in, from monolithic pattern to diversified consistency. Clearly, this is a period in which dangers abound. In the all-out *Umwertung*
that takes place, a diversification of social forms cannot yet be welcomed as riches, but only (or perhaps, primarily) as confusion. Consequently impoverishment of sociocultural organization types may first be
sought as a sort of countervailing source of strength, regardless of the
consequences. Again, the U.S.S.R. is an exemplary case.

But lest the argument be carried away by misgivings, let realism take
its place. A great deal is said these days about the dangers inherent in
such a situation, particularly regarding the threatened misuse of the
power thus created. As if there were yardsticks to measure misuse of
power in any given situation! As though the underlying urge towards
re-orientation, in whatever direction, were not the really significant
thing! What really matters, after all, is that societies whose isolation has
just been broken, or which hitherto merely vegetated, are now showing
signs of vitality. Whosoever realizes this fact will not wonder at the
dangers incurred, even though these may justly be cause for anxiety.
Under the given conditions, is not everything a matter of life and death?
Even so, there is some deep truth in the idea that development policy is
in a way also diversification policy.

(3) DIFFERENTATION NOT A CONSISTENT PATTERN

Next, a thesis closely linked to, and to a certain extent a repetition of,
the second, although from another viewpoint and expressed in other
terms.

The societal diffraction that is characteristic of underdevelopment
does not yield a consistent pattern.

An examination of the various segments of an underdeveloped society
in their togetherness does not result in a composite picture, if merely in
the broadest terms. It does not provide a view of a totality as made up
of its components, regardless of the manner in which the components
are conceived: whether in terms of social stratification, division of
labour, formation of public opinion, or any other. The several social
identities found in an underdeveloped society do not feature as elements
constituting a comprehensive social identity. So far as the latter really

deserves the name "identity", it is clearly inconsistent, not easily recognizable, often overstressing one of its aspects with notable disregard for the many other aspects which join in defining it. In short, prospective and sought-for rather than manifest and recognized identity.

Entities by themselves rather than effective components

To give a few examples: there is not one elite but many potential elites, with all the consequences that this plurality implies for the concept "elite". There is not one intelligentsia but many, and the several worlds of knowledge on which they base themselves have little or no relation to each other. Mass formation, whether spontaneous or even consciously encouraged, is dramatic in such a way that a thorough reconsideration of the meaning of the Western word "mass" is needed in order that one be able to get an idea of the significance of the masses – again in the plural – under conditions of underdevelopment. There are classes and there are also other categories of ranking, but none of them have a clear social function and significance, whether for members or for outsiders. The same goes for the relationships between one and the other; supposing then that such relationships exist, which is not always the case.

Such differentation-without-cohesion typifies the discontinuity which is so typical of the state of underdevelopment: not merely discontinuity signalling that at the particular time and place underdevelopment occurs, but also discontinuity in the long run. The survival crisis already mentioned is a perpetuation crisis, even if, like in the case of the name Ghana, it may imply a somewhat surprising reinterpretation of early history.[7]

An underdeveloped society can scarcely be considered a sociocultural continuum. Its differentiation does no longer, and at the same time not yet, add up to any kind of pattern that is characteristic of the society in question as one society. Its diversification is, for the time being, obscure, both as to its cause and as to its objective. Underdevelopment is at once incipient chaos, and emergent urge towards (re)integration. If development policy is diversification policy, it must at the same time promote cohesion. (Not necessarily the same as homogeneity: this matter will be taken up below.)

---

[7]   The present country of Ghana is named after a 10th century empire of rather different geographical features. Comp. P. C. Lloyd, *Africa in Social Change* (Harmondsworth, Penguin, 1967), p. 28.

(4) SOCIAL CONTROLS INADEQUATE

Given the types of social organization which are characteristic of under-development, the following noteworthy fact arises. The exercise of the social controls pertaining to these types of organizations is subject to impoverishment and delay. The latter, in their turn, correspond with the degree to which a particular type of social organization achieves predominance (see the second thesis).

Social controls erratic

Crucial is once again the characteristic of the in-between phase. A traditional culture pattern has perished, leaving only residues; a new culture pattern emerges, but as yet rather in the form of a need for a pattern than as a readily perceptible and distinguishable pattern. Accordingly, on the one hand, remnants of social controls occur that are unclear not merely as to what precisely they are effective for, and also as regards the speed and accuracy of such effectiveness. On the other hand, but not seldom interwoven with these, new or renewed social controls occur: to which the same uncertainties apply. In either case the nature and effectiveness of social controls is again a matter of "no longer and not yet". They are erratic and uncertain.

Span of control uncertain

The conditions applying to social controls in general, also apply to span of control. Remember that the horizon for any sort of social control, *i.e.* the limits within which a given system of social control is effective, will correspond with the loyalty horizon (or, if loyalty is stratified, or at any rate differentiated: loyalty horizons): that is to say with the scope of the particular social identity with which people will identify. In enforcing one specific frame for loyalty, such as the nation-state, development policy risks failing its aim either by overshooting or by falling short. The effectiveness of control exerted by those effectuating the development policy is bound to reflect this.

Control and the nature of authority

These general considerations apply more specifically – and often more dramatically – to power and authority as explicit and institutionalized forms of social control. Both the *modus operandi* and the legitimation of power/authority tend to be critically affected by underdevelopment conditions. Consequently, it is fairly normal for two contrary phenomena to occur more or less simultaneously: competition, often extreme and ruthless, between pretenders for the available power/authority roles, whether individuals or groups, and on the other hand an inclination on the part of those in power/authority to overassert themselves (and thereby to become subject prematurely to the law of diminishing returns).

As regards its operational modalities, note that the main lack of clarity does not lie in undue stress on one aspect, such as the political or the administrative, combined with relative neglect of other aspects, such as the cultural or even the economic. Rather it stems from the almost inevitable neglect of effective feed-back. Centralistic orientations, so typical for underdevelopment and neo-nationalism, are characterized not merely by a tendency to operate along lines of one-way traffic from centre to encompassing society at large. What is more, this centre-to-periphery pattern will tend to be perceived – and operated – as a top-to-bottom pattern. And as regards the one-way model, there is as a rule little attention for spontaneous feed-back, let alone willingness to create and maintain feed-back patterns. In overasserting themselves, those in control are only too apt to mistake for real feed-back the sham allegiance that one can foster by means of mass media and mass demonstrations.

Authority without roots: the dearth of feed-back

What makes this so much worse is that there appear to be reasons why one cannot really blame them for it. For lack of anything like an informed and structured public opinion – more precisely, for lack of anything like effective participation by the common man in public affairs – it is only too probable that the signals one could receive by way of feed-back would appear meaningless. If so, self-purposive power and absence of public opinion would constitute an effective vicious circle.

However, this line of reasoning, if carried thus far, seems to contain an element of falsification. After all, the independence movements that in so many underdeveloped countries have preceded the effective status of underdevelopment, could not have been successful without some measure of effective feed-back from common man to leadership. In many cases, independence has interfered with this feed-back, to the extent that new channels and new modalities of expression would have to be established, but have not been established. In their absence, authority in newly independent states risks showing a number of traits on account of which one could blame them, with justification, for not being basically different from colonial rule. The crucial problem of authority and power exertion in underdevelopment situations is how to create effective feed-back, lest those in control end up in a situation of "daddy knows best", which for all practical purposes is a situation of power operating as self-purposive, of neo-colonialism.

Does feed-back depend on education?

Until quite recently – and to a considerable extent even today – the matter of feed-back from public opinion tended to shape up as an educational problem. Correct as this may appear at the purely verbal level, it is a misrepresentation for all practical purposes: where is the educational system that will produce effective citizens? If education were the only answer, prospects would be very dim indeed, and nothing really could prevent regimes from overasserting themselves and from becoming, in fact, self-purposive. Fortunately, the omnipresent development urge could prove decisive in the connection: no regime can expect to last that does not somehow achieve some measure of development. And development without increased participation by the common man in public affairs is unthinkable.

For present purposes, however, this latter consideration is not helpful at all. In begging the question concerning goals and evaluation, it throws the argument back on its point of issue rather than helping it forward. What remains crucial, therefore, is the need for effective feed-back as the corollary to the exertion of power/authority.

(5) COMMUNICATIONS ERRATIC

Yet another sociological factor of underdevelopment makes its appearance in conjunction with the lack of diversity among available types of social organization, and also with the inadequate integration among the components of which the underdeveloped society consists. This concerns the society as a complex, system or network of communications: communication both of material and of spiritual goods, the latter referring particularly to information. In this connection, the society can be considered internally, as a unity within which communication takes place and spiritual and material goods are distributed. It can also be considered externally, as a sociocultural entity in itself which is connected with other societies by means of all kinds of communication. An underdevelopment situation is one of erratic communications in all respects. The traditional system of communication and distribution operates imperfectly, in fragmentary fashion. With respect to the kinds of things that can be communicated and distributed, its effectivity is handicapped in a manner that has nothing whatsoever to do with its traditional characteristics and inherent limitations. At the same time any newly emerging communication and distribution potentialities are incoherent, eclectic in their operation, and segmentary; they are not adjusted to each other or to anything else. In a way, therefore, there is a paucity of communication means, amidst much confusion; and consequently, scarcity of communicated goods, whether material or spiritual.

Conflict as a variant of communications: erratic and inconclusive

Of particular interest is that *mutatis mutandis* the same applies to conflict phenomena, their modalities and points of crystallization. The traditional causes of conflict, types of conflict and modalities of conflict procedure, have lost much of their relevance. New types become available only haphazardly, and are extremely difficult to exploit owing to the lack of consensus. Note that all this is so whilst there are more occasions for and possible matters of conflict now than at any other time or under any other circumstances: is there anything at all that is not likely to cause trouble during a period of *Umwertung aller Werte?* Indeed one is induced to believe that conflict material (another type of sociocultural energy in need of a purpose) must be mounting up, owing to the lack of regularizing modalities of social conflict. On the other hand, if and when it occurs, conflict is likely to have insufficient cathartic effect.

The absence or ineffectiveness of established rules for conflict has one interesting advantage, namely that conflicts and even revolutions tend to cost less blood than when a system of rules of conflict is in full vigour. The reason may well be that bloodshed requires, somehow, the justification of a metaphysically founded system, even if it were for example a mob that would be shedding the blood. Bloodshed is always sacrifice. For lack of such a justification, the impulse to go to such an extreme as bloodshed remains undirected and inconsequential, so that even complete revolutions can afford the relative luxury of being bloodless. Wherever there is an oncoming new orthodoxy involved, however, chances are that it cannot afford such luxury.

(6) PROVISIONAL CONCLUSION

Together, these five propositions do not yet provide a full sociological conspectus of underdevelopment. For present purposes, they need not. They should, however, be sufficient to suggest a number of "anticipated necessities": issues that theory tells you to expect, societal problems likely to occur under development conditions. The response that will, or will not, be given to these issues is much less a matter of general theory, inasmuch as it is bound to be conditioned, to a large extent, by the specific case in which it will occur. Allowing therefore for a range of possible responses to each of these likely issues, one can maintain nevertheless that what has been listed here is one category of valid pointers to certain constituent elements of the goal setting process inherent in development. As such, they are necessary ingredients in any effort towards evaluation of development.

11

PERSISTENT FRAME OF REFERENCE

From a discussion of "anticipated necessities" as apparent to the socio-logical approach, the argument shifts now to the other side of the picture, the inductive establishment of clues towards the identification of development goals.

To this purpose, the Middle Eastern culture area will serve as a case in point.[1] The discussion will follow the distinction, applied above, between effective residues and emergent tendencies. More precisely, the presentation will reflect the threefold distinction that, in the scheme above, is presented in the right column by way of elaboration of the basic distinction in two. Thus, one part will be given up to (a) persistent (part of) frame of reference (this chapter), another (b) to felt needs and manifest tendencies (chapter 12) and a third (c) to manifest necessities, including actual urges, problems and challenges (chapter 13).

This chapter, on the persistent (part of a given) frame of reference, will consist of (1) some introductory remarks, followed by some observations on (2) the ontological perspective, on (3) philosophical anthropology, that is, the prevailing vision of the human condition, and on (4) the nature of prevailing institutionalization.

---

[1] In the following sections a briefest summing up is attempted of ideas developed more fully, albeit less systematically, on earlier occasions. Comp. my *Mens en vrijheid in Indonesië* ('s-Gravenhage, Van Hoeve, 1949), Ch. III; *Cross-Cultural Studies, o.c.*, Ch. IX; "Traditional Images of Man, Society and State as Determinants of Development", *Conspectus*, I/2 (New Delhi, 1965), pp. 32-51; "Muslim Attitudes towards Planning", *International Yearbook for the Sociology of Religion* (Köln, Westdeutscher Verlag, 1969), in the press; "Middle Eastern Economic History: Some Background Considerations", rev. art. *History and Theory*, VII (Middletown, Conn., summer 1968), pp. 377-384; "Iranian Development in Sociological Perspective", *Der Islam*, 45 (Berlin, 1959), pp. 64-80; "Economic Development in a Sociological Perspective, Some Comments on a Case Study Concerning Iran", *Annali del Istituto Universitario Orientale di Napoli*, XVII/4 (Napoli, 1967), pp. 277-313.

(1) INTRODUCTION: CLASSICISM

One reason why the Middle East provides such a good case in point for present purposes is precisely its classicistic vein. Before discussing this feature it may be useful to quote G. E. von Grunebaum's brief and lucid definition of classicism, given with special regard to the Middle East.

Classicism as a cultural aspiration may be analyzed as having four constituents: (1) a past (or merely an alien) phase of cultural development is recognized as a complete and perfect realization of human potentialities; (2) this realization is appropriated as a legitimate inheritance or possession; (3) the possibility is admitted that the present may be recast in terms of past (or alien) perfection; and (4) the aspiration of the past (or the alien culture phase) is accepted as exemplary and as binding on the present.[2]

Classicism, in other words, is one way in which a given sociocultural entity may perceive itself. But when we speak of perception, we must be careful not to overlook its perfectly dynamic implications.

A society's self-view, when occurring along classicistic lines, may occasion tensions and perhaps action, whether on account of the awareness of something persistently relevant, in other words of an actually valid model that demands to be implemented ever anew, or on the other hand on account of the awareness that the existing state of affairs does not meet the standard of a given ideal, whether past or alien. If past, one may speak of orthogenic classicism; if alien, one may perhaps call it heterogenic.

Curiously, the most fitting catchword for thought and action in the former case will be something like restauration or revival, whereas in the latter case it could be revolution. More curiously still, this shows that the term revolution if used in a classicistic context is much closer, basically, to such phenomena as restauration and revival than will mostly be assumed by the Westerner who reads about revolutions in the Middle East.

By way of illustration, take the case of the conflict between the Jamāl 'Abd ul-Nāsir government of the United Arab Republic and the Ikhwān al-Muslimīn movement. The Ikhwān are, quite typically, a case of fundamentalist revivalism, of extreme orthogenic classicism. Confronting them, the Nāsir government stood and stands for a culture image that, insofar as it aims at a new culture, represents a classicism of a vaguely heterogenic type. The clash between the two, however, stems not so

[2] G. E. von Grunebaum, *Modern Islam; The Search for Identity* (Berkeley, Calif. U.P., 1962), p. 73.

much from opposing types of classicism represented by either: this is no more than a ready rationalization for the basic conflict. The basic conflict lies elsewhere: the two are competitive in having, each, to be an *ad hoc* orthodoxy in the sense discussed above. The obverse position, of a clearly heterogenic classicism opposing a vaguely orthogenic classicism, can be found in Kemal Atatürk's adoption of Western models in his effort to do away with the messy aftermath of Ottoman reformism.

Returning to the dynamic implications of classicism, we must elaborate somewhat further on the apparent ambivalence between feeling of guidance and feeling of inadequacy. Clearly, this is a matter of considerable importance under conditions of (under)-development.

The given paradigm and its efficacy

Whether as effectively followed guideline or as measure of man's everlasting shortcomings, the norms or paradigms implied in classicism constitute the clearest possible, and perhaps the only valid, case of *indépassabilité*, of effective residues whose effectiveness is upheld as a matter of principle. Classicism is nothing if not a pre-established response to the challenge of the moment, of any moment.

To state this thus categorically is one thing; to see what it may mean in practice is quite another thing. Turning one's attention to this side of the medal, one will find it useful to set out from the realization that, under conditions of classicism like under any other conditions, there exists a mutuality of perspective between the model image that a given sociocultural entity upholds to itself (and in the light of which it perceives itself) and the actual state of affairs that it represents (in various fashions) to the (various) members. What is typical of classicism is the inclination to accord primacy to one of the two components of this mutuality, namely the model image. Classicism is overstress on the pre-existent paradigm.

Under conditions of (under)development one is therefore likely to run into either of two possible complications. Either there will be competition, overt and critical, between classicisms: that is, between model images each of which is postulated by some to be the (exclusively) valid form. We have just seen two examples of such a situation. Or, on the other hand, there will be a crisis caused by the awareness that in the mutuality of perspective between model image and actual state of affairs the primacy does not rest where it should be, namely with the model image. Actual conditions are felt, or feared, to constitute an upsurging tide that threatens to sweep away everything of value. This is far from making these actual conditions more acceptable or, for that matter, from placing people in the best position to deal with them.

Either way (and even more so if and when the two occur simultaneously), conditions of (under)development are virtually bound to occasion fierce clashes between culture philosophies and their respective protagonists, and accordingly to cause a virtually desperate awareness of crisis. Note that, if anything, the introduction of such a novel and alien technology as mass media has contributed quite considerably to magnify and exacerbate these very phenomena. The havoc wrought by radio and tv broadcasts (no need here to mention place names of transmittors) must be seen and felt on the spot in order to be believed. In this respect, the much-quoted study by D. Lerner c.s. has not really begun to reveal the truth, simply because it turns a blind eye to what is being broadcast, and of what kind is the response thereto.[3]

The problems of legitimation

It is time to round off this section. We read nowadays quite a bit about legitimation of change. It is perhaps useful to point out here that in a classicistic context the legitimation of change constitutes the Achilles heel of development policy.

It would be of little use for present purposes to proceed now by an attempt to sketch the classical culture image of the Middle East; – assuming that it were possible to undertake such an effort.[4] Rather, the

---

[3]   D. Lerner, *The Passing of Traditional Society, Modernizing the Middle East* (Glencoe, Ill., Free Press, 1958). We sometimes omit to draw the most important conclusion from this kind of study, perhaps because upon first hearing it sounds so destructive and cynical. It seems important nevertheless to face up to what after all is neither cynical nor destructive but actually just disquieting and perhaps a trifle sad. The conclusion is that the more researchable phenomena are not necessarily the more important ones.

[4]   A few words should perhaps be devoted to the model image that has become specific to Islamic classicism: the golden age of Islam is the period of the four immediate successors to Muhammad, the *khulafā' ul-rāshidūn*. As a choice for a golden age, this period does not appear self-evident. Somehow, the early ʿAbbāsid period in Baghdād, the age in which Islamic civilization reached its peak, could seem to be the more likely choice. By comparison, the earlier period seems strife-torn, full of murder and warfare, thoroughly unsettled. Clearly, the fact that Muslims have preferred the period immediately after Muhammed must go back to other considerations than the ones implied in what was just said. In trying to trace those considerations, one comes up with the conjecture that the golden age of Islam can feature as the golden age because this was the period during which the culture revolution that was the signal feature of Muhammad's lifetime began to sort itself out. The period, in other words, during which became established the outline of what was henceforth considered to be the Islamic civilization, the Islamic way of life. Period, surely, that was still close enough to the Prophet's lifetime to be perceived as belonging to the orbit of his im-

attempt here must be to single out a few of its basic components. More precisely, it seems desirable to look for the ones that are most likely to exert a persistent impact because they are to the Middle Easterner what water is to the fish in the Turkish proverb: he does not know about it.

(2) ONTOLOGICAL PERSPECTIVE

The perennial ontology of the Middle Eastern culture area has one variant in Islam.[5] In the framework of Islamic thought, one can trace it in various instances. Thus, for example, Muhammad's basic message. Thus, more or less complementary hereto, concepts like *mujaddid* (the renewer of religion) and *mahdī* (the messiah returning at the end of time). Again, one may trace it in the sense of mission of men like Jamāl ul-Dīn al-Afghānī or Muhammad 'Abduh. More important perhaps, one finds it in the significance, for Islamic daily practice, of the *fatwā* (authoritative statement bringing an actual state of affairs under the vigour of a specific portion of religious law) and of testimony (the formalization of one particular state of affairs, out of the current flow of events, by someone who qualifies as a witness). Once more, one finds it in that other kind of witness (*shāhid*), the martyr (who upon laying down his life proceeds immediately into paradise without having to await the moment of last judgment).

The critical significance of the present moment, considered metaphysically

Take Muhammad's basic message again as one clear and relatively sim-

---

mediate impact. (The latter consideration ties in with the argument elsewhere in this essay: it is the period that signals the dynamic persistence of the critical "now" symbolized by the Prophet's life and mission).

[5] In order to rule out any possibility of misunderstanding it may be good to say here in so many words that in maintaining that Islamic civilization, specifically in its origins and inspiration, is part of the Middle Eastern culture area, no claim is made to the effect that Islamic civilization would be, or could be specifically, in the sense of exclusively, Middle Eastern.

The link between Islamic civilization and Middle East culture area has occupied various minds at various occasions, sometimes in a most dramatic manner. Its appearance has hardly ever been that of an established and accepted fact. Rather it has featured as a hotly debated, even contested issue. Thus for example, the clashes between Muhammad and the Jews of Medina. Thus, for another example, the *khātam al-anbiyā'* doctrine (Muhammad the culmination in an intermittent sequence of divine revelations), which is supposedly of Zoroastrian origin.

ple indication of the ontology that interests us. Muhammad has the mission to warn the people he addresses, that (1) the final judgment is imminent and that (2) it will spell doom to them unless they convert to a life given up to compliance with divine eternal law. The "here and now" is presented as entirely critical. It confronts man with God: with eternity, that is to say with the eternal law that is the true norm, the sense of existence.

This critical now does not primarily connote change and the fleeting moment between past and future, like it does to the modern Westerner. Rather, it connotes an almost contrary moment, and one certainly not lost upon Westerners, namely of choice as the signal feature of the fundamental human condition. The main difference between the Muslim and the Western ideas as here summarized is precisely that what to the Westerner is an alternative perception – based on the continuity of history and with the present squeezed in between the (weightier) past and future – has no equally important parallel in the Islamic context.

The philosophical elaboration of these basically religious ideas goes by the name of occasionalism.[6] Interpreting continuity as a sequence of isolated moments (more exactly, momentary acts of creation by God), it accounts for permanence as a variant of impermanence, and that without even getting trapped in anything like a dichotomy (Western fashion) of change versus permanence. This construct is fascinating precisely inasmuch as it represents the systematic maximization of the critical here and now. On the other hand, it has relatively little need of, or use for, elaboration of continuous time perspectives, whether retrospective (the past) or prospective (the future). It is not by chance that the typical form of Middle Eastern history writing is the chronicle.

Time-and-space perspectives: their relative significance

Considering the same matter at a more pedestrian level, one notes the "time perspective" of the common man as studied, for example, in one particular situation by Bourdieu[7] and in another, more or less by implication, by Peters.[8] The latter points to the "telescoping" that occurs

---

[6] M. Fakhry, *Islamic Occasionalism and Its Critique by Averroes and Aquinas* (London, Allen Unwin, 1958); L. Gardet, "La mesure de notre liberté", *IBLA* (Tunis, 1946).

[7] P. Bourdieu, "The Attitude of the Algerian Peasant towards Time", in: J. Pitt-Rivers (ed.), *Mediterranean Countrymen* (The Hague, Mouton, 1963), p. 55 ff.

[8] E. Peters, "The Proliferation of Segments in the Lineage of the Beduin of Cyrenaica", *Journ. Royal Anthr. Inst.*, 90 (1960), pp. 29-53.

in regard to past generations, a foreshortening of perspective in regard to the past. The former discusses the clear limits that obtain in regard to the anticipating that man can afford to undertake in respect of the future. The immediate future is more or less open to human anticipation, but the more remote future is decidedly out of bounds. Note that what applies to time perspectives applies with equal force to the spatial horizons to human existence, and this regardless of any distances covered in the nomadic cycle of movement.

The significance of all this for present purposes becomes clear in the following, quite customary question. How will people whose universe is ontologically and spatiotemporally determined in this manner respond to development needs: that is to the need for action, in the present, aiming at determinate goals in the future? Usually the question is treated as a rhetoric one. Is it not all too obvious that these people are not merely trapped in a vicious circle of disease, poverty and ignorance by the harsh facts of life, and that on top of this their basic philosophy prevents them from the very possibility to envisage alternatives? Is not, to them, fatalism the seal on a fate without prospects?

Fatalism: a false verdict

Upon closer inspection, it turns out that the matter cannot be shrugged off like this. For one thing, it is about time that Westerners should realize that the term fatalism does not apply properly to Islam and the Middle East. If, for example, Middle Eastern farmers seem to have a fatalistic attitude, it turns out that they realistically build on a good deal of accumulated experience and that the means to improve their situation are effectively beyond their grasp.[9]

Reconsidering the alleged Western time perspective

More important, in implicitly condemning the Middle Easterner's preoccupation with the present one tends to overlook that in the West (which inevitably stands model) we do not exclusively operate in the frame of a temporal perspective according to which time is a rectilinear irreversible historical sequence with the present a fleeting moment between past and future, potentially momentous only insofar as it may constitute the breaking point between the two. In fact, it is by relying on the alternate temporal perspective, the preoccupation with the present, that we manage to maximize the 'breaking point' nature of the

---

[9] G. Destanne de Bernis, "Islam et développement économique", *Cah. de l'Inst. de Sci. Econ. Appliquée*, 106, V/2 (Paris, 1960), pp. 105-146.

present: it is there that we introduce man the creator, who acts in regard to the processes of history and who attempts to mould the future, not necessarily according to the pattern of the past. Curiously, even McLuhan is in this regard less clearsighted than he wants to be.[10] One obtains the impression that he claims that it is only on account of electricity and mass media that things instantaneous have regained preponderance over things in the form of even sequences. This, it appears, is rather too intellectualist a reading of past and recent Western culture history, in that it seems to overlook the common man's frame of perception and action. It is, moreover, one-sided in that somehow it manages to disregard the profound Promethean urge in Western man, which, even if it aims at the future, has the present as its base. Notwithstanding this, his argumentation remains interesting insofar as it does point out how the contemporary West, in veering back to a measure of preoccupation with the present regardless of future connotations and prospects, appears to be getting somewhat closer to what has always been, and still is to a very large extent, characteristic of the Middle East (and, let us be sure to add this), what it was itself prior to becoming modern.

The historical continuum as a frame of reference

On the other hand, this turn of events cannot provide an excuse for anyone to disregard the time sequence viewpoint. If the restrictive preoccupation with the present is customary in the Middle East and becoming fashionable in the West, this does not mean that thinking in terms of a historical continuum [11] has been, or could be, given up by Westerners and can be dispensed with by Middle Easterners.

What is more, there are signs that even if the Middle Eastern preoccupation with the present, the critical now, is by no means losing ground (and how could it, under present critical conditions) there is an emergent awareness as to the complementary viewpoint. D. Lerner *c.s.* have chosen to call it increase in empathy. There is a clear increase in numbers of those effectively thinking and operating in spatial frames that are not necessarily limited by actual personal experience (whether individual or accumulated by generations). In this respect, a modality of vision and action that has always been restricted to a small elite is

---

[10]   M. McLuhan, *Understanding Media, o.c., passim.*
[11]   Note that this distinction has nothing whatsoever to do with the distinction between long run and short run, as customarily used in economics.

spreading over ever more people. On the other hand, one notes the increasing readiness of many who share the present urge towards betterment, to account for the lapse of time that is needed in order that efforts made will yield the desired fruits. In most cases this is still a far cry from effectively anticipating, and working towards, future developments. So long as no conspicuous, epoch-making philosophy comes to accompany the process of fundamental reorientation involved, the trend is bound to remain vague, and the pace slow. But even vagueness and slowness may have their reward, namely in the absence of overt, destructive conflict.

Development policy as improvisation

Under conditions like these, development policies undertaken by governments and other agencies of the Middle East are likely to appear to Western onlookers as haphazard, improvised, stop-gap policies. Most illustrative in this respect is the step-by-step nature of Egyptian economic and land reform policies as described by O'Brien [12] and Saab,[13] respectively. It appears as if only after a certain move has been made, those concerned can get ready to consider the next move. A side effect, of tremendous importance no doubt, is that in this piecemeal process of *gouverner sans prévoir*, the already discussed tendency emerges to mistake (virtually self-purposive) expansion of control by the central powers, into ever more remote recesses of society, for increased effectiveness of development policies.[14]

This judgment is not incorrect. Indeed Middle Eastern policies tend to be overtaken by the course of events. But as a judgment it risks being too rash and too harsh. We must not forget that, in being inspired by an overly Promethean, no doubt idealized, Western self-view, it risks to overlook the fact that development is to a quite considerable extent "lived through" rather than "produced". Man is part in it prior to, and more than, being in control of it. The Middle East attitude tends to be remiss in not consistently carrying control to the optimum. Thereby, it is perhaps safe from the typically Western temptation to try (and fail) to maximize it.

---

[12] Patrick O'Brien, *The Revolution in Egypt's Economic System: From Private Enterprise to Socialism, 1952-1965* (London, Oxford U.P., 1966).
[13] Gabriel Saab, *The Egyptian Agrarian Reform, 1952-1965* (London, Oxford U.P., 1967).
[14] The main complaint of Norman Jacobs, *The Sociology of Development, Iran as a Case Study* (New York, Praeger, 1966).

(3) PHILOSOPHICAL ANTHROPOLOGY

In the Middle East, theological-philosophical anthropology, in other words the persistent interpretation of the human condition and of human nature, is the corollary to ontology. Man is creature. Two orders of being make up the universe: the divine and the human. Distinct and distant, the two orders are yet related. The link, crucial to the human self-perception, is the recurrent theme of both theology and philosophy. In the context of Islamic thought, it appears in various presentations, such as creation, last judgment, and revelation as responded to by law fulfilment. There is no need here to repeat that the entire conception is a-historical. What is important here is that the God-man relationship has its necessary corollary in the relationship between man and fellow man.

In all this, there are two points that deserve attention in the present connection. One refers to the social dimension of human religiosity; the other to the interhuman implications.

The social frame for religion

As regards the former, formal religion [15] tends to be institutionalized in perennial bodies believed by their members to comprise (the true) mankind. Cultic in its manifestation, it appears in stylized overt behaviour and signified intentions on the part of its adherents. For all practical purposes, this means that it features as a full pattern of culture. The self-sustaining nature of formal religion tends to be underscored by the existence of a special category of persons whose activities, sources of revenue, access to information and occasionally also proximity to the centres where power is wielded, are entirely connected with the operations and maintenance of the religious community concerned. Crucial in this connection is that the religious community is a full way of life, the shape of the true humanity. In other words, it is the self-evident

---

[15] Informal religion tends to be less elaborately institutionalized. It will occur on a smaller scale than formal religion. It will be particular rather than universalist, restrictive rather than expansive. Its cult, although not basically different from that of formal religion, will be local rather than universal; its ambition need not necessarily and explicitly be perennial. Formal religion, rather than antagonizing or condemning informal religion, will tend to embrace it in the fold of its own catholicism: but there are limits beyond which heresies will be exposed and treated as such. Thus, the distinctness of the two is unlikely to wither away in the course of time.

natural framework for any thought or action on the supra-individual, societal plane.

Now this could hardly become problematic so long as there would exist only one religious community in a given sociocultural space. It would then effectively fill that space: being not merely "church" but at the same time polity, economy, culture and what not. Indeed, this is what basically the *umma*, the community of Muslims, is supposed to be. However, much as it has established predominance in the Middle East, the *umma* has never had the available sociocultural space all to itself. It has always had to share it with a number of lesser, mostly pre-existent, religious communities (which, by the way, had much the same basic characteristics as the *umma*). The so-called minorities (the term is not very fortunate) are an intrinsic part of the Middle East. More important and more awkward, the *umma* has, in its capacity of the sole human community, never succeeded in superseding that older and in certain respects more primary sociocultural entity, the kinship unit, as the true human community. On the whole, Middle Easterners have had no tragic difficulties in coping with the ambivalence between these two competing types of human community. Their experience in this regard antedates Islam by centuries.

Competing frames of reference for societal action

However, in consequence of developments occurring during the last century and a half, two further kinds of true human community have joined the competition for the Middle Easterners' allegiance: the Arab nation, and – plural phenomenon, this one – the modern state-nation. In the Middle Eastern perception, either will reflect some of the basic features just discussed with respect to the *umma*. In addition, either has further attractions.

In consequence, two fundamental difficulties affect any goal setting for development in the Middle East. The one refers to the true nature of the sociocultural entity, the community in which man will be able to lead a truly human existence: a question that could never be more acute than under present conditions of revivalism and quasi-revolution. The other refers to the apparently inevitable choice between four competing formulas for the natural unit of development.

Probability of pluralist "formula"

The choice may not have to work through elimination: Muslims have managed for centuries to work the ambivalence between *umma* and kinship unit. But if the way in which they have done so is to be useful as an example, the apparently all-out competitive relationship between the four will have to be toned down quite a bit. This will necessarily imply a – tacit rather than explicit, occasional rather than purposive – narrowing down of the extreme comprehensiveness of each, in favour of preponderance of certain of its aspects or features that prove particularly beneficial or constructive under given circumstances.

This slow process is hampered rather than furthered by a good deal of customary inter-Arab politics, where the moves back and forth between national, Arab and Muslim frames of reference are dictated by expediency (often on negative grounds: distracting attention from trouble) rather than by clear purpose.[16] The main disturbing factors would seem to be that any move from any national base to the Arab or Muslim frame is bound to be seen by anyone not operating from the same national base as an attempt at self-aggrandizement at the expense of others. It is obvious that this state of affairs has immediate and grave implications for any goal setting towards development.

Meaning and purpose of human relations

Turning now to the interhuman dimension, one notes that human existence is supposedly purposeful not merely transcendentally but also on the interhuman plane. Fulfilment of human existence in the latter regard takes the form of compliance with divine law, in respect of fellow man. The Muslim is supposed to admonish his fellow man to do what is approved and to withhold him from doing what is forbidden. Perhaps to an extent under Byzantine influence, this line of thought finds something like a culmination in the idea that those who qualify, in formal respects as well as in terms of access to information and to wealth and thus in capability to wield power, are naturally placed to occupy themselves with public affairs; virtually to the exclusion of those who do not qualify.

The two variants of human existence

In the connection, one notes the occurrence of what for all practical purposes are two distinct variants of the fundamental human condition; and in this matter, the distinctness as such is not one bit less important than the characteristics of either. In the one variant, one meets the ac-

---

[16]   Comp. Premier Gamal Abdul Nasser, *Egypt's Liberation, The Philosophy of the Revolution* (Washington, D.C., Public Affairs, 1955), pp. 84-87. To the three "circles" mentioned above, a fourth is added: Africa.

cumulation of leisure, seigneurial status, virtual monopoly (for the group but subject to competition between its members) of access to information, wealth and power. In the other variant, one meets the accumulation of endless toiling with no fruit, of ignorance, poverty and disease. No doubt, the line is drawn too sharp; but if one does not begin by drawing it too sharp one may miss it altogether and thereby overlook one of the crucial motive forces behind the contemporary Middle Eastern development urge; – and also overlook some of the basic reasons why the underdog does not revolt.

The common base of their outlook: subsistence

What blurs the line is not primarily the occurrence of a broad range of highly varied intermediary categories. Rather, it is the circumstance that between those on the one side of it and those on the other, there are certain quite fundamental things in common. For lack of an adequate name, one may try to sum them up in the word subsistence.

In its usual meaning, the word refers to the poor farmer who, since either the weather or the landlord will take away anything beyond the bare minimum for his survival, cannot be bothered to step up his productivity. In the meaning in which the term is proposed here, it stretches so as to embrace even the landlord, who does not know better than to take his ample share if and when he sees the opportunity. What the subsistence farmer and the "subsistence" landlord, and everybody else in the same sphere of thought and action, have in common is the inability to envisage maximization of effort as the means towards all-out betterment; [17] the idea that the landlord may fare better if the tenant

---

[17] Comp. R. Firth (ed.), *Themes in Economic Anthropology* (London, Tavistock, 1967).

How alien the idea of maximization of returns on effort really has to be, however, remains to be seen. One hears talk about expropriated landlords who manage to step up the productivity of whatever land is left to them to such a point as to avoid real loss in income. If and insofar as this information is correct, it suggests that under particular circumstances the real income aspect of the landlord's customary "subsistence" pattern can acquire enough significance in its own right to become instrumental in engendering something that is purposive maximization of the result of effort, even though there is as yet no "philosophy" underpinning it. Pursuing this line of thought somewhat further, one arrives at some intriguing speculation.

It is no secret that in many cases land reform has an alleged and a real primary goal. The former is betterment of agriculture and of rural conditions. The latter is to break the political power of the landlords as an entrenched reactionary clique. On the other hand it is generally recognized that expropriation and redistribution of land raise virtually insoluble problems of management of

is better off is completely alien to either of them. Obviously, the same will apply, although perhaps not necessarily to the same extent, to the craftsman and his employer. And the businessman, who is perhaps the least subject of all to the subsistence viewpoint, is precisely for this reason the object of the constant watchfulness of those in power.

---

agricultural enterprise and of agricultural extension work, and that they may in effect run counter against the need for increased size of agricultural operations.

Given these considerations, one looks forward to the moment when those in power will overcome their fear of the landlords and feel free to tackle the core problems of agriculture and of the countryside without prior, potentially distracting, concerns. This could lead to a very different appreciation of expropriation as a means for agricultural and rural betterment, and also to a very different stand to be taken in regard to the landlords. Imagine a policy that would treat landed property as held by landlords (with or without reparcellation between landlords) as so many agricultural enterprises in the "modern" sense: with full consideration for optimum returns on effort for all concerned and with adequate awareness as to matters of productivity. The landlord would find himself under the necessity to operate as owner-entrepreneur and might have to acquire expert help for the purpose. In all this he could be made to pass the threshold of hesitation or unwillingness by applying the necessary legal or political pressure.

In consequence of such a policy, the yield of the enterprise could be expected to increase considerably. There should be adequate arrangements to make sure that tenants and other workers receive their fair share ("fair", no doubt, by other than subsistence standards) in these profits, and so would the owner-entrepreneur and his staff.

In addition, there would be a fair margin available either in the way of tax for purposes of redistribution of national income or (perhaps: and) in the way of more or less compulsory investment in enterprises in other sectors of the economy.

In the process, the gradual change in nature of the agricultural enterprise could be expected (and if necessary would have to be made) to reflect in an equally gradual, yet irreversible, shift both in the relationship between landlord and tenants-labourers and in the nature and degree of the latter's participation in general well-being and public affairs.

In further consequence, one would hope the underlying attitudes both of the landlord and of the tenants to adjust to the new formula that is more or less forced upon them. This reorientation may be prompted (if it is done carefully), in the case of the landlord, through the influence of the expert personnel in his service (who could at the same time maintain some sort of relationship with the official agency promoting and controlling the entire operation), and in the case of tenants and labourers through adult education, agricultural extension and further services, whether as part of the operations of the agricultural enterprise concerned (but again with some links with official agencies) or provided from official sources.

As compared to the system currently applied in several Middle Eastern countries, this approach would have the tremendous advantage that it does not ruin the often quite effective working relationship between landlord (or representative) and farmer (and if ruined it is seldom replaced by anything else), but rather continues it whilst gearing it to a new purpose.

Subsistence is non-development

Curiously, certain aspects of development policies seem entirely fit to make sure that no break-through in the system would occur on the side of the businessman or the industrial entrepreneur: prevailing credit arrangements keep him safely tied to those in power. This may have the advantage that the potentially disruptive effects of a sudden break-away from the subsistence pattern, on the part of commerce and industry, is cushioned off. On the other hand, by slowing the pace of the movement away from subsistence and towards maximization of effort, other risks are taken that must not be underrated.

What has been said just now is a crude summing up of some of the observations made by Jacobs in regard to Iran. For situations like that of the United Arab Republic, one would have to complete the picture by adding that there, the government attempts to function as the motor and vehicle for an all-embracing move from the subsistence pattern to that of systematic maximization of effort. The example followed is, no doubt, the U.S.S.R.; but the philosophy that was in the U.S.S.R. instrumental to the purpose is rejected, nor is there a substitute for it. And the philosophy, in the last resort, is a matter of anthropology. So long as no substitute is effective, one must count that the millennia old anthropology of the Middle East remains one determinant of change and development.

(4) NATURE OF INSTITUTIONALIZATION

Both ontology and philosophical-theological anthropology reflect in something that merits consideration in its own right as a determinant of goal setting under development conditions: the nature of institutionalization. The point here is that much as institutions tend to supersede one another in the course of time, and particularly in times of upheaval such as the present situation of (under)development, they will mostly tend to be variations on some underlying, persistent theme. What matters, therefore, is to trace some of the signal features of that largely hidden theme, whether they be principles of organization or something else.

Organization never maximized

It is possible to detect one glimpse of these phenomena in the *umma*, which in this respect is perhaps more of an open book than many other

Middle Eastern communities of primarily religious inspiration. Given a full codex of revelation, it hinges, in the last resort, on a consensus that has been left intrinsically and operationally undefined. Its head is naturally the head of state; but the function has continually caused difficulty, again for lack of adequate formal provisions. At times, this state of affairs has come near to imperiling the continuity of Islam; and nowadays the *umma* persists notwithstanding the fact that the khalifate has been vacant for numerous years. In its turn, the cult of the local community is directed in random fashion: the function of *imām* is in principle fulfilled in *ad hoc* manner. There being no room for a priestly function, one finds scattered semblances of clerical roles and status; thus for example the *'ālim* (plural *'ulamā'*) or *mulla*, who teaches the disciplines of religion in a mosque or in his own school; thus, again, the judge.

Authority central, urban and self-maintaining

With the judge, one crosses the vague border between more typically religious and more typically political organization. In the Middle Eastern empire, of which the Islamic realm is one variant, institutionalization occurs by and large in the form of a concentration of power and authority in one centre of gravitation and in the person of one bearer. It is complemented by the geographical dislocation of his relatively loyal, personal representatives on various levels.

In the higher echelons and particularly at the top, the bearer of authority is the nucleus of the elite which, as stated, has the monopoly of access to information, wealth and power, albeit on the basis of mutual competition amongst its members. The elite, although typically urban, is recruited not merely from the town but from the village (landlords) and the desert (tribal chiefs) as well. In the old tribal system, which for a long time has somehow stood model for Middle Eastern political organization in general, authority has tended to have the more of an *ad hoc* manifestation, the higher the organizational level at which it occurred. Its self-continuation at the top level (the desert empire) has always been the main temptation and the main hazard.[18]

Some of these basic features are reflected in the crucial problem of continuity in the traditional Middle Eastern polity. The main fear of king Ibn Sa'ūd, the last Arab ruler of the classical type, was what would

---

[18] Comp. my "The 'Tribal' Sector in Middle Eastern Society: A Profile", *o.c.* (above, Ch. 3, n. 3).

happen to his succession. This point is so crucial that, conversely, stability, if and when it occurs, is bound to entail the danger of stagnation.

The contemporary Middle Eastern states continue their own variant of this crucial institutionalization problem. In fact, it goes now to the unprecedented extent that President 'Abd ul-Nāsir could succeed himself overnight. Let nobody mistake this for a case of almost disrupted continuity. It is in fact the worst kind of discontinuity, as it is bound to hamper the Egyptian nation's mental recovery from the sudden blow of military defeat.

Homogeneity not a vital consideration

A third feature of Middle Eastern institutionalization is the relatively little use it has for homogenization. For Westerners this is not an easy matter to comprehend. They have been brought up within the context of the European nation-state, which is assumed to be a homogeneous body in all important respects. The assumption goes to the extent that non-homogeneity is alleged to be a matter occurring across national boundaries, and that its manifestations within a given nation-state are obfuscated. How far this will go appears in the United States philosophy of the melting pot, and its incredibly slow withering away so as to make room for more realistic and more fertile conceptions, in terms of plural ethnicity and the like. By contradistinction, the Middle Eastern conception has never been cast in terms like these. Traditionally (and to an extent even to-day if one considers the Middle East – or, say, the Arab nation – as a whole), Middle Eastern society is a convergent society. It is a society that, whilst basically complex, is held together thanks to the circumstance that its components have a common orientation – and to an extent a common allegiance – to the culture elite. The specificity of components is determined by a range of functional and qualitative criteria; but its verbal expression tends to hinge on the qualitative ones.[19]

The culture elite functions as the mainstay of society, *inter alia* in such a manner that its self-continuation is at the same time maintenance of the society as a whole. The culture elite stands for, embodies, what the entire society purports to be, regardless of the specificity of each of its components. In their turn, these components are for all

[19] As compared to the functional ones in the case of a Western-type society where integration works through homogenization rather than through convergence.

practical purposes self-sustained and self-perpetuating (sub-)universes in their own right, perhaps even to the extent that internally they reflect the complex pattern of society at large, including culture elite and the rest. If they could be called minorities, the justification would rest mainly on the circumstance that their outlook would be somewhat less catholic than that of the encompassing society.

Issues: elitism with participation, integration with complexity

Now here is a perspective that in a development context proves most intriguing, but that at times may appear fully confusing. As argued above, development is, amongst other things, increased interaction. We have seen that whereas to the Western mind steeped in 19th century ideas this is bound to mean increased homogenization-*cum*-expansiveness, contemporary Westerners are beginning to realize that it may, in fact, have to mean increased integration through any viable means, whether homogenization or otherwise. As yet, there may not be too many development experts who are willing and able to envisage the implications of this "or otherwise". Having discussed some of them in connection with the problem of the natural unit of development, we should at this point have relatively little difficulty in envisaging the probability that in a Middle Eastern context the vehicle and instrument for integration may have to be increased interaction within some convergence framework rather than homogenization.

The main difficulty in the connection is clearly that Middle Easterners themselves are caught half-way in between the 19th century Western line of thought, which after all has been a major impulse toward their revival,[20] and the need (and perhaps desire) to rethink and revalidate their own approach to matters like these. The point is the more intriguing inasmuch as, like was discussed above, the trend in the West seems to be away from the maximization of integration, towards something perhaps not too different from the Middle Eastern appreciation of complexity as a thoroughly workable proposition.

The crucial question is, of course, who will bring about what kind of convergence using what kind of instruments. In the connection, it is worth noting that in certain Arab circles there exists an interest in the operational pattern of the European Common Market. Again, as a

---

[20] Albert Hourani, *Arabic Thought in the Liberal Age, 1798-1939* (London, Oxford U.P., 1962).

formula, the Arab League represents a most interesting venture, even if its path is beset with all sorts of difficulties and even though its success in certain respects is continuously blurred by its impotence in some other, allegedly more important, respects.

12

FELT NEEDS

This chapter, on felt needs and manifest tendencies, will be introduced by (1) some remarks on the Western impact as a triggering factor. After that, with the sociologist's predilection for subject matter worth presenting under the present heading, some observations will be made on (2) the nature of diffraction of sociocultural reality into units, and on (3) the interplay between the resulting units.

(1) INTRODUCTION: THE WESTERN IMPACT

It is often thought, and with reason, that if underdevelopment situations show the double tendency to eliminate the West and to emulate it, the Western impact must be the sole or main triggering factor in the development urge. The purpose of this introductory subsection is simply to serve warning against too categorical an interpretation of this thesis. In the Middle East, the Western impact has been – and still is – quite varied; in addition it has had – and still has – diversifying consequences in certain regards.

Western impact not uniform

To see how varied it has been one need only recall that whereas the Maghrib and Sudan have for all practical purposes been effectively colonized, Iran and Afghanistan, Turkey and the Arabian Peninsula have not. The remaining countries are somewhere in between. The curious consequence is that, for example, relatively few Iranians appear to be ready to consider Iran as an underdeveloped country but relatively more Tunisians are prepared to think of their country as being in need of development and to make an effort accordingly. Conversely, insofar as the latter are perhaps somewhat more outspoken on the matter of development goals, they will at the same time incline more towards

Western ideas and standards, as they see them. Nothing is permanent in this regard, however, witness the manner in which the pendulum has swung back, in Turkey, from extreme attempts at westernization to a more balanced orientation.

Again, there has been considerable variety in the preponderant aspect of manifestation of the Western impact. In the Maghrib and Egypt, it was commercial before it could become political; in the Levant it was at one time cultural-religious prior to becoming political; along the Persian Gulf coast and further North it was vaguely commercial before becoming all-out technological, not without political implications. Speaking of technological impact, it is obvious that the uneven distribution of natural resources has been dramatically underscored, for example by the exploration and exploitation of oil, and the particularisms of the traffic pattern by the Suez Canal. There is, moreover, an equally uneven distribution of the revenues from these resources and of their impact on the wider economic systems concerned: but this is not necessarily a matter of Western impact alone. In the same manner, population growth, and the move of population from the desert into the sown and from the countryside into the town, cannot simply and directly be attributed to Western impact alone. However, just like in the proverb all roads lead to Rome, so all these various impulses are bound to reflect in social change in its various modalities.

To Middle Easterners, the West is not one bloc

Behind all this lies an even more intriguing consideration. Unlike any colonial territory that necessarily experiences "the West" exclusively through one nation-state, namely the "mother country", the Middle East as a whole, and most of the separate parts of the Middle East, have, ever since the Crusades, been facing a plural and divided West. Moreover, the West thus experienced was originally something else than mere colonialism or imperialism.

This has two important consequences. One, what would appear, at one time, as (belated) colonialism and imperialism, has been, at an earlier stage, the fundamental antagonism between two complete ways of life, based on mutually exclusive religious tenets. This can only mean that in the last resort, colonizability, to use Bennabi's term again, is in the Middle East basically different than in other areas. And so must be, consequently, the eventual reaction to (the later forms of) colonialism. On the other hand, the mutual competition between Westerners (including, no doubt, competition between Russia, later the

U.S.S.R., and Western Europe, gradually replaced by the U.S.A.), is a natural ingredient, according to a Middle Eastern viewpoint, of the relationships between Middle East and West. Non-alignment in the Middle East is therefore basically different from neutralism in India (but perhaps not all that different from certain leanings in the Yugoslav position).

Concluding, if the urge to eliminate the Western presence is as strong in the Middle East as it is in most (ex-)colonies, it may nevertheless involve less inferiority feelings and accordingly more self-searching. If the urge to emulate the West is visible in the Middle East, the imitation of the Western example, which could appear inevitable in certain African countries and in situations like Indonesia, is likely to receive less accent than the elaboration and assertion of a historically continuous selfhood that should be in all respects a match to the West.

(2) UNITS OF SOCIETAL DIFFRACTION

There are various ways in which the diffraction pattern of Middle Eastern society seems headed for modification. So far as one can see now, this refers primarily to the nature of some of the component elements. Insofar as it expands into the interaction between such components, it yet need not affect the basic non-homogeneous modality of diffraction that was said above to be typical of the Middle East. The present subsection will deal with some of these components, not entirely regardless of the way in which they interact with one another. The next subsection will deal with the interaction proper, but not regardless of the components thus interacting.

Attention here will be focussed, selectively, on (a) sex and family, (b) the mob, and for slightly more elaborate discussion (c) "social strata".

a. *Sex and family*

One of the discontinuities that are notable in the Middle Eastern culture area refers to the sociocultural manner of accounting for the biological datum of sex difference. The traditional image of man is for many purposes split up into two entirely distinct variants, the male and the female. By closely paralleling varieties in religiosity, this duplication of the image of man acquires a considerable measure of persistence. There is a man's world and there is a woman's world.

Man's world is to a large extent the same as the public sphere, public affairs. This is at the same time the sphere where the man (not woman) of independent means engages in public affairs in the sense of the religious cult, economic action and, in the last resort, politics in the full, original sense of the word. The public sphere has a variety of manifestations, ranging all the way from the ruler's audience hall, to the bazar and its shops, to the café and the street corner. Each of these is a more or less institutionalized, specific extension of that basic manifestation of the public sphere, the street.[1] Note that public office derives its meaning and connotations from the same context. Indeed, the office, in the sense of a location where an official transacts his business, is essentially a public place – witness the pleasant tradition to offer any caller some refreshment. The office, in the sense of the official's occupation, is for the same reasons a capacity, a status, a matter of authority, of exerting power as a person (rather than as a functionary or, tell-tale word, public servant).

Woman's world, on the other hand, is more private and sheltered, more based on persistent relationships and restricted circles of (oral) communication. The distinction between the two worlds may extend into the dwelling that serves as the common home for both man and woman: a door or even something as flimsy as a curtain will mark inexorably which parts are accessible to male visitors and which are not. And if woman moves outdoors, the curtain moves with her; a veil or shroud keeps her sheltered even in the outdoors. Consequently, a woman who acquires a so-called modern education and who wants to apply her non-traditional skills is misplaced by traditional standards. She has to move into the public sphere which is defined as exclusively male. By the – to her and others – obsolete standards of tradition, she purposely conducts herself in an undignified manner. If some emancipated or semi-emancipated women in the Middle East appear somehow tragic, there certainly is ample reason. This however will not stop their number from increasing, nor from making tradition undergo rather important changes. These will somehow affect the very nature of the public sphere and of office, and in the last resort of authority. It looks, moreover, as if the only way in which the identification between one of the sexes and a particular complex of social roles may become undone is in a roundabout manner, namely by detaching role from (male) person, in other words by depersonalization and functionalization. This latter point will come up for some further consideration, below.

[1] By comparison, the North American street is no man's land. The circulation it conveys is instrumental not purposive.

At the same time, the male – and in consequence also the female – role in the family is likely to change. Contrary to what may appear to be the case at a first blush, chances are that the male role will lose in sharpness of definition and that in consequence it might broaden some-what in the long run. The cause would lie in the expected blurring of the public sphere: if this is no longer the exclusively male domain, and if in consequence the male is no longer identifyable as part of the public sphere, something may change in the family. Rather than having the neatly circumscribed role of head and ruler of an (extended) family that, however, for most daily affairs does not need his effective pres-ence, he may find himself a member, in a vaguer but broader sense, of the (nuclear) family. Whether this will entail increased participation, rather more on a par, in the affairs of the home is anybody's guess; but one need not exclude the possibility of some slow changes in this direc-tion. What is beyond doubt is that as the family becomes less and less extended, to the point of being nuclear, its economic autarchy abates and therefore its relationships with the wider community and the fami-lies therein are bound to change. The crucial question in this connection is whether any mutual participation can emerge, and if so, of what kind and for which purposes. Problems of security are bound to loom large in all this, and their implications and repercussions tend to be widely ramified.

b. *The mob*

The disproportionate expansion of cities, particularly of capital cities, during the last decades has caused various changes in the urban pattern and in urban-rural relationships. Some of these will be discussed below. What deserves attention here is the phenomenon of the mob. It is usual-ly, but somewhat too easily, identified with the rabble of the streets that is a millennia-old urban phenomenon, not merely of this particular culture area. The mob, in its acute manifestation, is an utterly destruc-tive tidal wave of human beings who are temporarily together under a common high emotional strain. What is novel is that nowadays the togetherness is organized and the strain induced by manipulation of selected mass communication techniques. What is also novel is that these outbursts (which go by romantic names like "black Saturday") are instrumental towards the achievement of goals which as such are sub-jects of cool calculation, usually on the part of politicians. Not that these politicians would be ready to identify with the mob in action: rather they resort to it as a kind of extreme gadget for surprise use.

The mob is a terrible thing and a dangerous weapon in many ways. Perhaps the worst about it is that it can be used to reach a sham cathartic effect: like the fake pregnancy in Huxley's *Brave New World*, it is made to serve as a fake revolution: absolving those who claim the need for revolution from going all the way, and safeguarding them from the risk of being devoured by a real revolution. In its present form, the Middle Eastern mob is pending like a Damocles sword over a good deal of public activity in the area, not excluding action in favour of development. It is the weak spot in urban reconstruction (in the social, not the physical sense), and it is a crucial element in the (re)patterning of social strata, that is to be discussed next.

c. *Social strata*

The inherited stratification pattern consisted, broadly speaking, of (1) an urban culture elite recruited from and rooted in town, village or desert, with a virtual monopoly of access to knowledge/information, wealth and power, (2) the broad categories of commoners, whether urban, village or nomadic, and (3) various in-between categories, mostly of an urban nature.[2] Flexibility in this pattern was largely a matter of social mobility of individuals and their families. Likely candidates for the purpose were the desert hero, the successful farmer-proprietor and the unusually successful merchant. By definition and in respect of their interrelationships, these broad strata are not classes in the usual sense of the word. Class-consciousness as stressed by Marxian and post-Marxian philosophies is by and large absent, except perhaps in the elite.[3]

The continuation of this pattern is not likely to occur without modification. It is actually under stress from various sides. Basically, it is affected by development: the urge towards increased participation by all appears incompatible with privileged access for a few to some of the main values in life. More visibly, it is affected in two ways.

The upsurge of in-between categories

The quantity and range of in-between categories is increasing, due to the impact of so-called modern education and to the introduction of modern production systems with corresponding patterns. Besides, in-

---

[2] For details see my *Social Stratification and the Middle East* (Leiden, Brill, 1965).
[3] For a refreshing, avowedly Marxist, approach to class phenomena see Hassan Riad, *L'Egypte nassérienne* (Paris, Minuit, 1964).

sofar as there exists something like a revolutionary trend in the area it is directed against the traditionally established power elite. Note, however, that it could well be that in being so directed it is, more specifically, taking aim against a particular, exclusive group of wielders of power rather than against the elite phenomenon as such. This observation, subtle and seemingly academic, is in fact of considerable pratical importance. We shall return to it below. Note for the moment that several of the in-between categories, such as intellectuals, officials, officers, are visibly candidates for the elite role. Nor are there any clear signs that, were they to achieve it, they would be loath to take advantage of some of the privileges it may entail.

Ideology and stratification as the key to the distribution apparatus

It may be interesting to envisage this general state of affairs in the context of actually operative forces, for example, nationalism or syndicalism. Each of these, in trying to build strength on ideology, stands for a more or less outspoken ideal of stratification. In fact, to their adherents the realization of a particular stratification pattern may well appear instrumental towards achieving development as they propose it. Thus, syndicalists' thought may somehow be affected by the model of the proletarian revolution: to the extent that they might attempt to foster an effective proletariat which, by revolting and taking over control of society, would prove a means towards the realization of their ideal society, – no doubt as the norm for development. In the same manner, certain brands of nationalists may feel that a budding middle class, with some vested interests and some entrepreneurial spirit, could provide the preconditions for self-sustained growth.

There are at least two reasons why one should not overrate the importance of views like these. One is the length of their chain of reasoning and the somewhat hypothetical nature of their premiss, *i.e.*, the emergence of a particular class (of very Western definition). The other is the finite nature of the same chain of reasoning, as compared to the basically infinite nature of development. Once more or less achieved, a particular desired stratification pattern would be bound to continue as a conservative proposition, and thus to hamper further development. In practice, this danger is even less remote than it appears in theory. Already in several Middle East countries certain newcomer groups (embodied in parties, juntas or otherwise), once having achieved control over society by ousting or emasculating the traditional power elite, find themselves promoting essentially conservative aims: precisely to the extent that they can hardly afford to conceive of themselves as an intermediary stage in, and as instrumental for, an ongoing development process, the ultimate implications of which remain to be seen. Instead, as monopolist manipulators of development, they almost inevitably cut it to their own measure.

Elites: necessary leverage for societal action

This leads the argument back to the point already mentioned in passing: the significance of the succession of elites as power wielders. Two points deserve attention. The first is that, critical as stratification may appear in a development context, it yet cannot offer an effective hold for those intending to effectuate development not merely as a matter of shock treatment: by means of one or a few hardly related forcible impulses, – but as an ungoing concern. The point is that they risk getting trapped, long before they know, in a state of affairs where their recipe for social stratification is short-circuited somehow with the existing situation. From then on, their effectiveness as change agents is finished.

The second consideration, reinforcing the first, is that in the Middle East stratification may, after all, not be as crucial to development as outside observers, with their Marxian and post-Marxian preoccupations, may be inclined to assume. What really matters is that which lies underneath stratification, and to deal with which stratification is, in the West, considered to be an effective instrument. It is the control over and distribution of information, wealth and power: that eternal complex of which scarcity seems to be the main feature according to human perception. No doubt, the Western way to deal with this complex, and to effectuate necessary reshufflings in its regard, is by manipulating the stratification pattern. Or at least, so it seems since Marx and since we have started reading the history of the French revolution backwards in a Marxian light. There is no reason why in this regard the Middle East should conceptualize and act in conformity with the current Western vogue. In fact, upon some reconsideration of the traditional Middle Eastern pattern of social stratification, one arrives fairly readily at the conclusion that the struggle for the elite position may not have all that much to do with stratification as a comprehensive societal phenomenon.

Stratification as a comprehensive pattern may not have critical significance for development

If so, most of what has been said thus far refers actually to one limited phenomenon, not unusual in the area, that in its present appearance is symptomatic for social change, and which may or may not be conduvice to development, rather than to development proper. For purposes of goal setting it may accordingly prove ephemeral.

Thus, with an inevitably longish detour, the argument returns to the question from which it set out, namely concerning societal diffraction, as exemplified in stratification, and more specifically concerning the importance of social strata and what goes on in their regard as possible clues for goal setting in development process.

As said above, the traditional pattern of social stratification in the Middle East is not a class pattern in the usual, basically European, sense. It so happens that nowadays a good deal of the talk and action concerning development in the area is phrased, more or less vaguely, in terms of class models. Nevertheless, it does not appear likely that changes occurring in the foreseeable future would turn the Middle Eastern stratification pattern into a class structure. For one thing, the current scrabble for elite positions is against it. For another and more important thing, the implications of the development urge are against it. Recall that this urge, in stressing increased participation as such, is likely to foster egalitarian models rather than hierarchical ones. In its light, a stratified class model is as good or bad as the traditional Middle Eastern pattern: the one has no attraction over the other.

Probability to elitist egalitarianism

We now have two crucial considerations. One is that what really matters for development is control over the distributive mechanisms for information, wealth and power (and perhaps the reshaping of such mechanisms for the purpose of control). The other is that on account of the social justice content of present orientations in the area, such models as will be operated must be susceptible of being presented as egalitarian. The holders of control, whether passing in quick succession or successful in maintaining themselves, will be in no position to afford conspicuousness as a distinct class, even though they will certainly be an elite. What is most striking in this prospect is that it is so close to the classical Arab ideal of authority, with its typical blend of consultative authoritarianism and condescending accessibility. If present developments will cause deviations from it, these will mainly ensue from the impact of mass communications: from the immediacy with which rulers and effective citizens will be involved in one another's doings.

Avoid easy assumptions about a middle class

In consequence of the same factors, one may perhaps anticipate an increasing range and variety of in-between categories, not nearly all of them potential candidates for the elite position. As a further consequence, the boundaries between in-between range and top and bottom categories may become increasingly blurred, and the bottom strata lose in numbers and in clarity of specific characteristics.

In terms of goal setting, these prospects may catch less of the limelight than some of the more doctrinaire positions briefly referred to above. Even so, chances are that they may prove more important in the long run.

(3) INTERPLAY BETWEEN COMPONENTS OF SOCIETY

The present section is given up to a brief discussion of societal diffraction in the Middle East as demonstrated in the interaction between some selected components of society. There will be first (a) a few introductory remarks delving somewhat deeper into the phenomenon of diffraction as it occurs in the Middle East. Then, some attention will be paid to (b) minorities and nation-states, and after that (c) to the relationships between town, village and desert.

a. *Nature of societal diffraction*

It may be helpful to consider somewhat more closely the nature of societal diffraction, that is, of the manner in which a given sociocultural entity, as a form of unity, is composed out of various sub-entities in meaningful relationships with one another. In order to understand the specificity of diffraction in the frame of the Middle Eastern culture pattern, the Western observer can hardly avoid making comparisons involving himself. In comparing the nature of diffraction in the Middle East and in the West, one seems to find that they differ. Whereas it is a primary phenomenon in the West, it is secondary in the Middle East. In the Middle East it presupposes (and in its firmly rooted culture elite effectively refers back to) a given ultimate truth that is commonly assumed to be the common base of all humans. The modern and contemporary West, on the other hand, operates thus far [4] on the basis of

---

[4] A question arises in this connection, due to current changes in the West. The common non-truth has proved so effective a base for all kinds of thought and action that it cannot be considered any longer as radically different from the

ad hoc verities, which amounts to operating on the common assumption of the absence of a common bond of ultimate truth. Hence, the Western need for and ensuing maximization of homogeneity: as a corrective to the primary datum of diffraction. Hence, on the other hand, the Middle Eastern ease in living with non-homogeneity, which after all is necessarily and automatically convergence: diffraction being at root no more than variation upon one given theme. The implications are fascinating. Thus, on the one hand the Western need to conceive of conflict primarily in terms of conflict resolution: as against, on the other hand, the Middle Eastern predilection (and ensuing skill) for dealing with conflict in terms of conflict management. It is tempting to draw one further conclusion and associate the Western urge towards maximization of the result of effort with the expansiveness that is, in its turn, the corrolary to the need for homogeneity, and on the other hand to envisage a link between the Middle Eastern mosaic pattern and its subsistence orientation: expansive in its turn but for quite different reasons.

There is in all this a lesson for present purposes. What one notes here comes very near to being an effective residue of the kind discussed above. Diffraction and non-homogeneity are very much the same thing, in the Middle East. This can only mean that in studying the interaction between components of Middle Eastern society one will necessarily be concerned with the field of tension between, on the one hand, the inertia of the inherited diffraction pattern and, on the other hand, the urge towards more intensive communication that is the corrolary to development.

b. *Minority and nation-state*

As a fair illustration, consider the Middle Eastern minority and also the Middle Eastern nation-state.

---

position here described for the Middle East. Science, particularly applied science, is for all practical purposes firmly established in the role that in the medieval West and in the traditional Middle East has been held by revelation. The consequence could be that eventually the West may afford a greater degree of non-homogeneity than has seemed possible hitherto. This fact could have interesting political implications. Thus far, homogeneity was maximized in the framework of the nation-states, and non-homogenety was allowed to run wild in the no man's land between these states, where it could be disregarded. It is impossible nowadays to regard that which occurs between the nation-states as no man's land and accordingly as nobody's concern; but in order that effective conclusions may be drawn from this realization, other ways must be found to account for non-homogeneity as an actually visible phenomenon. The basis for such recognition appears now to be available in principle.

Terminological clarification

The term minority as used in regard to Middle Eastern conditions must be taken regardless of its most conspicuous connotations as currently debated in the U.S.A. It refers to any component of Middle Eastern society at large that comes near to having all ingredients for being a society, a full sociocultural entity by itself, and that on top of this differs from the over-all society (as maintained by the culture elite) in regard to some crucial, or at least conspicuous, features of the culture pattern. Most effective as a signal feature of difference is religion, but other criteria do occur. In fact, in most cases a main signal difference comes in the company of a broad range of supplementary differences, such as language, dress, professional specialization. Besides, a minority will tend to be separate in terms of location, occupying, for example, a town quarter or part of a village. If and insofar as minorities are at a disadvantage as compared to the majority, this is unlikely to be conceived, on either side, as automatically demanding immediate redress. Here lies one of the reasons why the term minority, which in its Western use does have this connotation (and necessarily so: the demand for homogeneity!), is a misnomer if used in regard to Middle Eastern conditions. It is not as if by redress of disadvantages minorities will automatically adjust and thus disappear. According to the traditional outlook, they are equally permanent as society at large.

The nation-state as a neo-minority

In the light of what has just been said, it cannot be difficult to see why the nation-state can be discussed along with the minority. They share most of the characteristics just reviewed. The main difference is that the nation-state is somewhat more emphatic in its being specific regardless of all the others. This is due to the fact that, unlike the minorities, it came into existence when the encompassing wider society, having been deprived of practically all effective institutionalization although by no means having disappeared as the ultimate frame of reference, had no way of keeping the expressions of the specificity of these novel entities (component entities, by its standards) within reasonable limits. The crucial point here is, clearly, that in this area the nation-state occurs within a wider framework that even if poorly institutionalized is indeed effective. This was much less so when the European nation-state was in its heyday.

Be this as it may, the main problem of the Middle Eastern nation-state is precisely that in postulating its sovereignty it is at cross purposes with two basic data, to which it lends a joint impact in the process. The one is the given fact that under contemporary circumstances the viability of any sovereign nation-state is questionable. The other is the already mentioned persistence of the broader Middle Eastern framework, which now finds partial expression in references to the Arab nation and in appeals to Muslim solidarity. Recall that appeals of the latter nature tend to go not unheeded even by Arab Christians.

Prospect: relatively less specificity and relatively more interaction

In either case what seems to be in store is a gradual decrease of visible specificity. This is due to the increase of similarity and of empathy, resulting from increased communication. Already one notices, in parts of the area, a tendency to conform with the majority in dress and in language. Professional specialization in minorities or kinship groups is losing ground at the same time, be it for reasons mostly of a technological nature. All this is quite clear in regard to the minorities. For the nation-state a similar process may be in store, but particularly in the near future it may be more difficult.

Note, on the other hand, that if exclusive specificity seems bound to decrease, it is yet unlikely to wither away altogether. In fact it appears likely that, modified and toned down both in regard to signal features and to function, they will continue to play a role. In the connection one is reminded of the concept of ethnicity as used by Glazer and Moynihan [5] in a study concerning New York. The gist of their argument, as it seems to apply to present purposes, is that the old competing ethnic groups, each representing a political-economic and to an extent (sub-) cultural structure all by itself, are gradually finding themselves components of an ongoing concern that, perhaps, will more and more become their common ground and that gradually may become institutionalized accordingly.

c. Town, village, nomads

Mutatis mutandis the same applies to the age-old triad of town, village and desert. Traditionally each of these is a full way of life in its own right. Their separateness is a major datum in Middle Eastern socio-cultural space. Even so it allows for, and in fact presupposes, a measure of interaction if not interdependence. But far from being maximized,

[5] Nathan Glazer and Daniel Patrick Moynihan, *Beyond the Melting Pot, The Negroes, Puerto Ricans, Jews, Italians of New York City* (Cambridge, Mass., M.I.T. Press, 1963).

these tend to occur in almost *ad hoc* fashion. Besides, such continuous importance as they may have refers to the elite rather than to the commoner.

The town used to produce and maintain culture, perhaps prior to producing material goods and an area-wide communications system that would convey goods as well as people and (or rather, with) information, plus a modicum of peace and order to maintain it. To these purposes it used to draw upon village and desert: taxes in money and/or in kind, conscription, additions to the elite being the irregularly contributed assets. Between village and desert the interdependence had a narrower base and tended to be more ambiguous. In the olden days raiding and sedentarization were somehow related, and trade either way used to have some quite shady aspects.

The development urge appears to necessitate a considerable increase in regular and effective interaction between the three. This may even have to reflect in matters of institutionalization. In addition to being culture centre, administrative centre and power control (including military and police) centre, the town needs to become service centre.

If it assumes this new function, this may go to an extent at the expense of the older ones. Besides, other factors are involved. Urbanization at the present pace is bound to lead to disastrous consequences. And so far as the nomadic way of life is concerned, the desert seems bound to empty out slowly but inexorably. Moreover, with regard to industrialization and to changes in agriculture, important decisions need to be taken in respect of the distribution of population over the available geographical space. Population increase, where it assumes significant proportions, is an additional factor of urgency in this connection. Lastly, there is an obvious need for the countryside, at least those parts of it which are inhabited or can be made fit for habitation, to be made livable.

Urbanization spreads beyond the town limits

At the present time, these various necessities add up in prompting a kind of effort that cannot constitute an adequate response in the long run. At best, it constitutes a first step, and a rather wasteful one. It is fairly common for central authorities in the Middle East to develop some concern, urban in its aspiration and elaboration, for the needs of the countryside. It has various expressions, ranging from more or less forcible sedentarization to land reform and to the promotion of co-operatives and other initiatives for association.

In its practical implementation, a good deal of this concern is translated into a continuous spread, in depth and in width, of the efficacy of central power, with political control as its main manifestation. Considered in the wider perspective just discussed, this tendency risks proving abortive. Yet, it is perhaps inevitable under the prevailing conditions. But even if that were so, nobody could really afford to take it for granted and to disregard its inability to meet some of the major needs. Once again, if it comes to the matter of development goal setting, the stated immediate goals are perhaps less important than the less conspicuous ulterior ones. But they do exert an impact.

13

OBSERVED NECESSITIES

The argument has now reached the point where, in the attempt to find clues concerning development goal setting, inductive and deductive ways come close. Under the heading of observed necessities two foci of interest will be singled out. For purposes of shorthand indication, one (1) may be labelled socialization of potential, and (2) the other functionalization.

(1) SOCIALIZATION OF POTENTIAL

Consider the two following statements, both repeatedly used in the preceding. In traditional Middle Eastern society the culture elite has privileged access (though on the basis of competition between its members) to knowledge, wealth and power. Development connotes increased participation of all (who make up the development situation concerned) in the full round of life and particularly in betterment of conditions. These two statements, each symptomatic for a full vision of sociocultural reality, are at odds: and this in two ways. Obviously, they contradict one another in that the one will afford to some what the other claims for all. Less obviously but at least as important, they refer to utterly different conceptions of knowledge, wealth and power.

Knowledge

The knowledge of the traditional Middle East, is, in the last resort, the complex that results from the full elaboration of revealed truth. Basically, it is given and perennial. Man's duty in its regard is first of all to treasure it and subsequently, in maintaining it, to apply it to actual situations. These, no doubt, will necessarily feature as object for the purpose. This kind of knowledge is typically the concern of a limited category of initiates, of a culture elite.

On the other hand, the kind of knowledge that is typical of the development urge may in the last resort connote ultimate truth, as an ever receding prospect. For all practical purposes it is operative behind the relentless effort of the mind to move from one *ad hoc* verity to the next. It will do so by maintaining an incessant interaction between the *ad hoc* verity of the moment and the (aspect of) reality to which it is supposed to be relevant.[1] Of course, in development situations the *ad hoc* verities referred to will mostly appear as *ad hoc* conceptions of what society should be like. The kind of knowledge that is involved here is necessarily everybody's concern.

Wealth

In the same manner, the concept of wealth (and the complementary concept of its counterpart, poverty) is according to traditional Middle Eastern ideas a descriptive category applying to the human condition as a given fact (namely in each individual case: the thought pattern is occasionalist). The two are merely variants, though quite contrasting ones, of one and the same fundamental human condition. Above, the term subsistence has been reinterpreted in an effort to bring out the basic outlook that links the two. Here, certain consequences deserve to be noted. One is that poverty is in itself not dishonourable, let alone a cause of despair. If and when it becomes desperate, the despair is likely to derive from physical rather than from moral considerations. (Even so, slums will be slums.) Another is that security is not primarily a matter of the absence of poverty. Of course, there is security in wealth that can be shared. But there is security also in shared poverty; – perhaps, in a way, even more of it, be it on an empty stomach.

Health

It is hardly necessary to add that basically the same considerations as apply to wealth and poverty will also apply to health and disease. Neither health nor wealth, up to whichever minimum degree, feature in the traditional Middle Eastern outlook as a normal need that

[1] Lest it appear as if the Western writer falls a victim to ethnocentrism in this passage, it may be useful to recall that, due to objectification as an instrument towards the development of the "scientific" approach to reality, a good deal of Western thought about development remains trapped in 19th century Western conceptualization. It does not take knowledge to be perennial but it does nevertheless take it as given and ready to be applied to, if not imposed on, a reality that for the purpose remains object.

would obtain for everybody. On the other hand, this is exactly what development is somehow hoped to achieve: liberation from the shackles of poverty and disease. In becoming sensitized to development, people begin to be aware – if not simply to hope or believe – that poverty and disease are not an intrinsic part of the normal human condition for particular, hereditary categories of humans.

Power

Similarly, once again, the matter of power versus powerlessness: of being in a position to command as against being in a position of having to obey. The development urge connotes a measure of participation in the conduct of public affairs for all. It does not necessarily connote that it must be the same measure for all, or the same degree of professionalization, or with the same modalities of institutionalization. This is why it is wiser to avoid terms like democratization in a connection like this.

Enough now of oppositions. So long as one considers it in terms of contrast, the matter is relatively simple and surprisingly clear. But as soon as one tries to envisage it in a perspective of development goal setting, let alone of viable development action, there is less occasion for confidence.

The common man's participation: the crucial issue

Under the circumstances, development action devolves on a particular group of nationals, who may or may not avail themselves of expert advice by foreigners. Let it be assumed now for argument's sake that such a group is entirely dedicated to promoting the cultural, political, administrative, social and political participation of all, as their way to effectuate development. Then, the probability is, and experience proves, that they are up against some major stumbling block precisely at the most crucial point of their proposed activity: their interaction with the rest of the nation. This is not merely a matter of their going too slow for some and too fast for others. The problem is more vicious.

Where an effective public opinion would be needed, if only to provide them with feed-back, it proves inexistent; and efforts to bring it about result, for the time being, in little more than either the hollow echo of a political claque (ominously amplified, at times, by the mob) or the negative criticisms of those who cannot or will not understand. Where associations for self-help would have to emerge of their own accord, the effort to create and promote them culminates, for the time being, in little more than endless extension of central authority, which moreover bestows an administrative-political hue on everything it touches. Where financial and/or technical assistance is pumped in so as to create increasingly numerous nuclei of viable economic action, its net effect is, for the time being, little more than to further enrich those already wealthy and powerful. Where modern education prepares white collar and blue collar workers of various kinds it will, for the time being, tend to yield little more than oversaturation of a few restricted urban labour markets, the brain drain taking care of any surplus of highly qualified people.

Elitism and the danger of self-sustained isolation

These things are bad enough by themselves. But they are worse inasmuch as there is no real hope that continued, and if necessary further expanded, effort of the same nature would be enough to break through the vicious circle. It may or it may not, and there is no saying how long it might take. And after all, time is important. The reason why there is no hope for gradual betterment is that there is a regressive impact involved. The elements of self-purposiveness and self-continuation that were just signalled as virtually inevitable under the circumstances, are dangerously similar to the self-continuation of the elite that in the traditional order was the effective and sufficient means to maintain society as a whole. With so little visible difference between traditional state of affairs and budding development effort, there is grave danger that not only the common man but also the (new) leadership will drift rather too easily back and forth across the dividing line. In other words, there is a continuous danger of relapse. Danger that is further enhanced by the somewhat overheated sense of unity that tends to be fostered by critical conditions and that will give those in control even more of a blank mandate.

What one observes here is a clear case of conditions leading, on the one hand, to necessary short-run goal setting but demanding, on the other hand, a particular kind of long-run goal setting: and this in such a manner that the two kinds of goal setting are completely at odds.

(2) FUNCTIONALIZATION

Turning to functionalization now, one finds that the matter is in no way different.

Personal capacity versus organizational function

In regard to knowledge equally much as in regard to power/authority, not to mention wealth, the traditional perception is that they are held and wielded in a personal capacity. In the same manner, social belongingness and political allegiance, even employment, are matters of personal relationships. Social groups are primarily kinship groups to which one belongs as a person, by birth. Even membership in *umma* or church, with its entirely different formal criterion of professed faith, proves in actual practice a matter of personal identification with a full way of life. A trade or occupation is a personal capacity in the literal sense and insofar as it is hereditary the personal element is thereby enhanced rather than obliterated.

The technological component of development is such that one anticipates the need for a fair degree of functionalization. This could hardly be limited to trades and occupations. Further repercussions affecting political roles and economic functions appear likely.

But again, any moves in this direction appear doomed to lead astray. The danger, to be sure, is not that depersonalization would turn out to be dehumanization, the way it did during the Industrial Revolution. This could perhaps be an ultimate risk; the real difficulty that is immediately visible is a different one. The problem right now is that in virtually all cases a beginning trend towards functionalization is stopped short in its very first beginnings, when it appears, provisionally, as depersonalization. What happens is that the personal holder of a role or function is ousted and replaced by (or finds himself compelled to metamorphose himself into) an official: this being the first step, in many cases, to do away with the past and to start moving towards the future. However, the official concerned will tend to operate according to an existing paradigm or frame of reference. Doubtlessly, in order to do his job well he would have to anticipate the fully developed conditions of the future in choosing a pattern of official action and behaviour to which to conform; and in so doing, he would actually help to create the pattern. To do so is hardly what pertains to any official capacity anywhere. The consequence is that the official will conform to the one and only known paradigm: that of the past. This is the paradigm that tells him to consider his official capacity in a personal light. Officialization, whilst meant to be a first step towards depersonalization and eventually to functionalization, may prove the reconfirmation, in the name of the new order, of the traditional outlook. A vicious circle of the worst kind.

Association: a novel type of social organization

Similarly, the introduction of associative forms of organization, to complement the traditional kinship-based forms, remains a matter of imposition. This is a contradiction in terms by itself; the consequences are even worse. Those who supposedly should start the association and build it up through some division of functions between themselves, actually find themselves taking orders, more or less passively if not grudgingly, from some outsiders in some role of authority foisted upon them in the turmoil of these chaotic days.

The two points are jointly illustrated in various situations of land reform where the landlord has been ousted and the conduct of affairs placed in the hands of some farmers' co-operative under official guidance.

The ideological vacuum

As a distantly parallel phenomenon of perhaps even more ominous implications, consider the ideological vacuum that signals the actual degree of secularization in the area. The personal influence of those in religious capacities (who, for lack of an established clergy in Islam, were never quite part of the ruling elite) has started to wane even prior to that of those belonging to the elite in other capacities.

Insofar as political leaders have wittingly or unwittingly stepped into the shoes of religious authority, they have done so without hesitation. Between the political and the religious there are no boundaries to cross. Indeed, even the apparently careless shifting from one frame of reference to another (nation-state, Arab nation, *umma*, etc.) comes perfectly natural inasmuch as fundamentally speaking these are identical anyway.

However, all this flexibility has yielded meager result. What they have offered amounts to non-alignment at the international plane and some mainly verbal, strenuously nationalistic-*cum*-Arabistic ideology not seldom styled socialist. Neither could serve purposes much beyond the self-perpetuation of these same holders of political power. Non-alignment, for one, has proven an effective device for distilling apparent power, both nationally and internationally, out of an international power vacuum in the area, fostered by manipulating the mistakes of the big powers in such a manner as to render them cumulative.

Now all this is not, or at least not in the first place, a matter of bad faith. It follows immediately and inexorably from the quite realistic consideration that if some group of people wants to effectuate development for society as a whole, their first need is to be, and to remain, effective. Once more, short run and long run goal setting do not match. In order to be able to set the indicated long-run goals as one sees them one is compelled to set short-run goals, the realization of which threatens to prove a step away from, rather than towards, realizing the long-run ones.

Conclusion

The intriguing aspect in what has been discussed under the heading "observed necessities" is that indeed the inductive and the deductive approach to clues for development goal setting do both apply in a way, but that they do not match. General and more or less theoretical considerations will lead you to look for one kind of goal setting. Realistic consideration of actual conditions warns you to count with the probability of quite another kind.

For purposes of evaluation of development, one would somehow have to account for the fact that two kinds of goal setting, here rather simplistically distinguished as short-run and long-run, are likely to occur, as well as for the fact that the two tend to be at cross purposes.

14

INTERLUDE

Let us see where we stand. In discussing the likelihood that evaluation of development will come to the fore in the next few years as a necessity in various ways, we have been thrown back on the need to know about development goals: these being the only valid yardstick by which to assess achieved development.

Summing up

In discussing goals, we have found that these can, and in fact must, be identified both deductively and inductively. Consequently we have seen that some goal identification is likely to occur primarily in general theoretical terms (with two ensuing needs, namely (1) to establish the relevance between goals identified in general terms and actual development situation with which one is dealing, and (2) to integrate the several goal identifications produced within the frame of reference of each of the social sciences and – applied – sciences). Another kind of goal identification is likely to occur primarily in specific terms applying to the particular development situation with which one happens to be concerned (with (1) the ensuing open question how much generalization this could bear, for example through comparison between various development situations, and (2) recalling the already discussed question concerning the natural unit of development).

On the basis of this primary distinction, a somewhat more refined distinction has been introduced, namely between types or orders of phenomena in which, or on the basis of which, one could expect to identify possible development goals. A fivefold scheme was the result, which has then been elaborated and illustrated in a manner that, if it does not recommend itself for balance and elegance, should at least have the virtue that it is realistic.

Of the two deductive categories, one has been left undiscussed here, namely the one that, starting out from the pre-existent fund of knowledge, concentrates on symptoms, indicators and the like as ensuing from existing theory in the various disciplines. The reason is that particularly in economics it is a major topic of current interest, covered in abundant and easily accessible literature. No need repeating. The other has been tentatively elaborated in terms of one of the social sciences, namely sociology. Obviously, full coverage of the two categories would require, first, elaboration in terms of all disciplines not mentioned now, and, secondly, integration of what the several disciplines would have produced in so doing. No attempt could be made here to do either. On integration something will be said below, but more will remain to be said.

As regards the three inductive categories – namely persistent part of pre-existent frame of reference, felt needs and manifest tendencies, observed necessities – the Middle Eastern culture area has been selected to serve as the specific unit of development within the framework of which to consider the identification of three categories of possible development goals. Some will feel that the chosen area is wide for the purpose; the problems that arise in this respect have been accounted for, as much as possible, in the course of the argument. Again, full coverage of the subject matter would require expansion of the work, in at least two directions. One is, obviously, other development situations, whether nation-states, culture areas or otherwise. Here again one faces the question of generalizability, perhaps through comparison. Some measure of comparison has been employed in the preceding, albeit merely as an explanatory device for Western readers. It could perhaps be systematically elaborated so as to become serviceable for purposes of eventual generalization. The main stumbling block on the way towards generalization would appear to be the sheer quantity of case material that would have to be processed and contributed.[1] The other necessary expansion of the work would refer to the predilection for a sociological viewpoint that has inspired the choice of illustrations used here. Complementary and corrective contributions from other disciplines would be indispensable. To this purpose, however, a collective work would have been required: perhaps a task for the future.

---

[1] The use often made of the well-known Human Relations Area Files serves warning not to put one's hopes too high if it comes to comparison – and ensuing generalization – on the basis of systematically arranged data on a considerable number of relatively large but widely different sociocultural units.

Goal identification: a starting point for further work

What remains to be done now can be summed up as two steps. One is to envisage what the consideration of clues towards identification of development goals can teach us in regard to the use of identified goals for purposes of evaluating achieved development. The other is to envisage how that which has been developed here relates to current thinking on development indicators and the like.

At this point it is necessary to make sure that the argument will not become entangled in some of the terminology in which it is cast. Particularly, terms like goals and goal setting must be understood as terms of convenience, regardless of some of their usual connotations. They have been used here minus the anthropomorphic and voluntaristic implications that the word goal usually has. In their present usage, these terms refer back to the theoretical considerations developed previously. They should be taken as virtually synonymous with other terms used before, such as emergent tendencies, focussing and the like. A development goal, as understood here, is one more or less distinguishable, *ad hoc* concentration or convergence point, one pointer in a particular direction, in an overall situation assumed to be largely in flux.

15

CONSPECTUS OF GOALS – PLAN AND POLICY –
EVALUATION AS FEED-BACK

Up to this point the discussion on the identification of development goals, lengthy as it has already become, has not moved beyond the first step, namely the identification, in a given development situation, of a number of separate goals. No doubt, this first step is crucial for whatever may follow afterwards. Still, what we have available now is no more than a foundation. What matters is to build on it.

From separate identified goals to conspectus of goals

There are two more steps to be taken. First, we can now consider in which way numerous separate goals identified in a particular development situation can be conceived as existing effectively together. Does the plurality of goals add up to some sort of unity? If so, it should be possible to determine in which sense a development situation shows identifiable trends: the *ad hoc* convergence of the preceding analysis. The present section will be given up to this second step. The idea is clear: the basically discursive procedure that seems to be characteristic of goal identification as discussed thus far constitutes a severe handicap if it comes to putting the fruit of all this labour to some use. The ever so many goals that one can hope to identify in the manner suggested make relatively little sense unless and until they begin to "add up": that is, until one manages to envisage them within the scope of one comprehensive overview, – a conspectus, in the literal sense. They need to be envisaged in their togetherness.

But before entering upon any further discussion of this matter, it is useful to point out that in a sense even this second step is instrumental, not purposive: namely as soon as one's aims go further than achieving a measure of intellectual grasp on a given development situation for academic purposes.

From conspectus of goals to plan and policy, then to evaluation

There is a third step that can, and quite often must be made. This leads from the assessment of the inherent trends and potentialities of a given development situation to either the act of development policy making (both planning and implementation of plans) or, on the other hand, to the act of evaluating development achieved over a certain span of time. The two are in no way mutually exclusive, and there is a tendency afoot to argue that the one is very much in need of the other. Before long, we shall have to make a few more remarks on this – double – third step.

The complex of goals

Returning now to the second: the problem of envisaging how any number of goals identified in a given development situation can add up so as to feature as the complex that will determine the development process concerned. In speaking of one process one commits the sin of over-simplification, no doubt; but this is not the occasion to let ourselves be thrown back on the earlier discussion of the natural units of development. What matters now is the one complex featuring as determinant. This is again oversimplification. Plurality of goals is involved, and also variety. Besides, interaction of goals is involved. Some tentative elaboration of both of these considerations seems appropriate.

A viable way of penetrating into the complexity of the matter is to deal with plurality and variety both at once, namely by considering them as the consequence of distinctions applying to the matter as a whole. Since most of what must be said in this regard rephrases, more or less systematically, things that have been said in the preceding analysis, it is possible to put the matter quite briefly.

Towards a typology of goals

First, a distinction applies between persistent and emergent goals, urges, trends, etc. The former represent, in a way, the continuity aspect in development: thanks to them, elements of the past remain effective, if necessary *mutatis mutandis*. The latter may be described as characterized by novelty: they are more or less exclusively related to the present and in a sense to the future.

Secondly, there is a distinction between goals, etc., that serve to keep prevailing conditions fit for given present purposes and those which, perhaps to an extent regardless of the present, refer to what is envisaged as becoming crucial in the more or less foreseeable future.

Above, this distinction was phrased as long-run versus short-run.[1] This is not simply a distinction into two. There is a complication. (Insofar as this is a matter of interaction on the basis of a given distinction rather than a distinction pure and simple, it should really be discussed in the next sub-section; but there can be no harm in anticipating.) As a rule, the short-run goals, both as mere goals and insofar as they determine action, will have an effect on the long-run ones; and vice versa. This effect may vary within an extremely wide range, running all the way from reinforcement to modification to suppression.

A third distinction runs between goals, etc., that turn out to be effective and those that prove ineffective or abortive. There is a risk that this distinction could become value-loaded. For example, interpreting it in terms like functional and dysfunctional would require extreme circumspicion. The point is that it is definitely not meant to run between constructive and destructive, positive and negative goals. Note also that the matter of effectiveness versus abortiveness is likely to elude contemporary assessment. By and large, it will be a matter of judgment after the facts, retrospectively. This point will demand some more attention below.

A fourth distinction, close to the third but not quite the same, refers to the duration of effectiveness rather than to degree or modality of effectiveness. It runs between goals etc. that wane in the course of the development process concerned and those that increase in effectiveness. This is again a range of possibilities, with steady effectiveness as the middle position.

On interaction between goals

As regards the complexity *per se*, its main characteristic is, naturally, interaction: what is complexity to a logical viewpoint is bound to feature as interaction to an operational one. What matters is modalities of interaction. Two considerations demand particular attention.

One refers to relative stress as between several goals. We may assume that out of several (kinds of) goals etc. that will feature in a given development situation, some will either persistently or temporarily prevail over others; and this to variable degrees.

[1] It is perhaps useful to point out that utopian ideals and the like, insofar as they feature as goals or tendencies in development, are not necessarily long-run goals in the sense of the second distinction. As a rule, they contain some element of short-circuiting between such long-run goals and the persistent impact of the past as featuring in the first distinction (allowing, of course, for corrective presentation of that past, which may go so far as virtually turning it inside out).

The other consideration refers to the probability that between existent goals, etc., no perfect harmony will exist. In the manner in which (and the degree to which) they will correspond to one another, there is bound to be a wide range of variation, all the way from concordance to disaccord. In considering the consequences one has once more to distinguish, namely between possibilities ranging, in the former case, from mutual reinforcement through disappearance of the one by becoming subsumed in the other and, in the latter case, from complementary through elimination of the one by the other. Taking the two ranges together one arrives at a set of three typical possibilities, including (1) complementarity, (2) mutual reinforcement and (3) zero joint effect. Of these, the latter is equally probable as the two former ones taken together.

The conspectus of goals

The two considerations together lead up to the query concerning the cumulative effect of the interaction. Insofar as effective development is supposed to result, at a given moment, in a relatively novel state of affairs, one must reckon that, by definition, this result corresponds to the cumulative effect of the interaction concerned. More exactly, the two concepts are different ways of looking at one and the same thing. The difficulty involved is that, again by definition, this cumulative effect can be perceived in retrospective fashion only.

However, for many this will not do. Recall what was said above about a third step having to follow after the second one, now under consideration. The obvious need of the development planner and policy maker and executive, is to anticipate it rather than to sit around and wait and eventually figure backwards. Even the scholar, whose concern would remain limited to this second step, would occasionally have little use for the time lapse needed to render retrospection possible. He would not necessarily encounter difficulties any time he would be working on some period in the past, but he would not suffer the present to be declared out of bounds to him.

In putting the matter in this manner, we may be holding a clue towards the solution of the difficulty. If there is a way out of this apparent deadlock, it should lead through gradually developing prognosticative abilities, on the basis of generalized insight that should in its turn be built on comparison of case material retrospectively interpreted.

Reading this, some will sigh and say that the way ahead of us is long and arduous. Others, for example certain economists, will smile and pity the writer for foolishly thinking that he is saying something new: are they not doing exactly this all the time? The trouble is that both reactions are correct. At the end of the road ahead of us (or, in case we would already have covered this road, right in front of us), we should find models at our disposal. Indeed, so far as one can see, models are the only way in which to deal with materials as complex as these. For the same reason, they would in all likelihood have to be mathematical. But on the same grounds why they have to be mathematical, they would also have to steer clear, to a considerable extent, from quantification. Not to all the things discussed above could one hope to apply quantification. It is perhaps particularly on account of the kind of quantification on which they are built that models nowadays show such a tremendous turnover. If it be true to an extent that available models are somehow the end of the road that some scholars found it necessary to cover, it is equally true that each model that becomes available is a milestone on the perhaps rather longer road that remains to be gone.

The uses of the conspectus of goals

At last we reach the third step. Let it be assumed now that with respect to a given development situation the various prevailing goals have been properly identified, and that they have been integrated into a conspectus that accounts both for their relative importance and for the way in which they affect one another mutually. Let us now discuss for the moment that this conspectus of development goals, insofar as it would be a momentary picture, is up for correction from one moment to the next.

The third step leads from conspectus of actually existing development trends – should one dare to call it pattern? – to development plan (*cum* policy) on the one hand and to evaluation of development on the other. In principle, one faces two possibilities in regard to evaluation: between actual development situation, as rendered intelligible in the conspectus just referred to, and evaluation of development, planning-*cum*-policy may or may not occur as an intervening phenomenon. The distinction is largely academic, however. Rare are the cases where an interest would exist in evaluating achieved development in the absence of an effort towards development such as is contributed by planning and policy.

An academic case: evaluation of development without planning

The proposition is in a sense simpler in case evaluation would be intended under conditions not involving planning-*cum*-policy. Indeed, it is tempting then to conceive of the operation in terms of comparative statics, on the basis of two momentary pictures assumedly differing on account of a time lapse between the two moments at which they were taken. This might even mean that one could suffice by producing two of the conspectus just referred to, and that one would not even have to bother whether they would be cast in terms of process or, more customarily and thus more easily, in terms of qualitative categories. As a historical research device and perhaps even as an educational tool, this procedure has proven merits.[2] It is likely, moreover, that its results would prove more significant, in terms of generalizability, the more one would succeed in avoiding some of the basic limitations inherent in comparative statics, namely by casting to two conspectus with which one will work in terms of process. The stress would then automatically shift from shifts in constellations of fact to shifts in operational modalities, which may be advantageous both theoretically and for purposes of gaining useful insight. Even so, the heuristic value of the device, and particularly its prognosticative use, remain doubtful. Besides, for the reason already mentioned that planning-*cum*-policy will hardly be absent from cases worth any attention at all, this particular approach is bound to remain largely academic.

What and how to evaluate if there is a development policy

The alternative is by one element more complicated. It would refer to conditions where plan-*cum*-policy do occur. According to customary reasoning (the validity of which remains to be considered), it would accordingly work on the basis of three elements: the already mentioned conspectus of development trends, the plan based on that conspectus, complete with its implementation, and a new conspectus after a certain time lapse.

A number of questions arise in respect of this presentation, some of them quite hard to answer. First, whether plan and implementation can be counted as one element for purposes of the present construct or not. Secondly, whether the conspectus referred to would be a dead momentary picture cast in qualitative categories or an image cast in terms of process and on this account constantly under revision. In the latter case,

---

[2] Comp. my *Society as Process, o.c.*, pp. 167-178.

there would be a third question, namely whether one could validly speak of two different conspectus. If so, a further question would arise, namely whether for purposes of analysis one would have to resort to freezing two variants of this flexible conspectus, so as to make each stand for a particular moment in time, with a chosen time lapse separating the two. This, clearly, would reintroduce comparative statics by the back door after it has solemnly been expelled by the front door. Another important question would refer to the norm for evaluation. Assuming that one would evaluate from the standpoint of the "second" conspectus, referring to the "later" moment in time, and agreeing furthermore that evaluating is basically the act of drawing conclusions from comparison, will then the base line or bench-mark for this comparison be the conspectus referring to the "earlier" moment or alternatively the plan plus ensuing policy assumedly based thereon?

Simplification: the construct of development agent in development situation

Upon closer consideration this entire range of questions appears to refer back to one fundamental distinction. It runs between the development situation as such, and on the other hand, the stated expression of human volition. The two are neatly distinct, but they are not unrelated. The latter is meant to be relevant to the former, not merely in terms of efficacy of volition but, prior and as a precondition thereto, as a meaningful presentation of it. There is yet a third link: policy implementation is in a sense nothing but interaction between the one and the other, mediated by the same human agent(s) who first distilled plan from reality.

One ends up in the well-worn construct of reality and image of reality, the latter at once meaningfully derived from the former and purposely imposed on it. But at this point the question must be raised whether the customary presentation of evaluation on a basis of planning and policy is correct. If these two acts are considered, in traditional fashion, as momentary acts standing in some sort of causal sequence, then there is bound to be a third moment when effect of imposition will be assessed, using "previous situation" as benchmark and plan as norm or yardstick. If on the other hand, the two acts are considered, in more process-like fashion, as simultaneously occurring aspects of persistent process, then the ensuing need for evaluation is, as a matter of principle, bound to shape up differently in its turn, namely as equally simultaneous feed-back: ensuing, for the agent concerned, from imposition of image on reality. Evaluation and feed-back are, then, fundamentally synonymous.

Evaluation: obsolete urge or new impulse?

Two conclusions follow. One is that the present fashion of increasing interest in evaluation of development is a carry-over from conceptions of development, both as process and as action, that are rapidly becoming obsolete. The other is that nevertheless the concern with evaluation, if duly translated into a concern with feed-back, is not merely legitimate but in fact marks a great stride forward, both in regard to sensible development action and in regard to theorizing.

Another considerable advantage in considering the matter in terms of feed-back rather than in terms of evaluation is that the former eliminates an undue and in fact most disturbing connotation of the latter. The idea of evaluation seems somehow to suggest the existence of an independent third party who will, by means of yardsticks of which he has the privileged disposal, sit in judgment on the performance of a given development agent in regard to a given object (that is, a given development situation). This indeed is what evaluation currently means. It explains at the same time why the use of evaluation should show such a notable tendency to be restricted to limited, and limited-purpose, projects with very clear goals,[3] and why even then the evaluation proper remains such a thorny and touchy matter.

Evaluation as feed-back

We arrive now at the following position, already anticipated in some of the preceding remarks. Development policy is at root a matter of steering, according to a course that has been set out with due consideration of everything involved. What matters is (1) the "consideration": in other words, the way in which the development plan is produced, given the development situation concerned, and (2) the manner in which feed-back is obtained and employed. Evaluation, taken in a corresponding sense, is the act of obtaining feed-back, usually with the intent that it be available for the appropriate use. The second procedure differs from the first in some important respects.

As regards the former, the road from conspectus to plan is arduous,

---

[3]   Comp. R. Hollister, *A Technical Evaluation of the First Stage of the Mediterranean Regional Project*, Paris, (OECD), 1967. See also P. Hesseling, *Strategy of Evaluation Research, in the Field of Supervisory and Management Training* (Assen, Van Gorcum, 1966), and D. Braybrooke and C. E. Lindblom, *A Strategy of Decision, Policy Evaluation as a Social Process* (New York, Free Press, 1963).

but its nature is fairly simple to describe. Crucial is eclectic maximization of elements, plus enforcement of consistency. There are two reasons for this: (1) manageability, both for intellection and for action, and (2) communicability, between those producing the plan and an optimal number of others constituting the development situation concerned. Again there are two crucial problems: (1) the norm by which to decide which elements to maximize and which to neglect, and (2) the degree to which it pays to promote consistency.

In either regard, it is likely that doctrinaire standpoints will be at loggerheads with rather more sophisticated and experimental approaches; what the former may gain in the short run they may lose in the long run, and the latter vice versa. For example, a doctrinaire communist standpoint may seem instantaneously to dictate the answers to issues that may crop up on the eve of a revolution; and so may the fundamentalist doctrine of groups like the Ikhwān al-Muslimīn in the Middle East. But as Chinese and even Russian history seem to suggest, this is no guarantee against a wavering and in many ways wasteful course over the years.

Feed-back in its turn is basically a reading of the deviations from the likely course of events pertaining to the process or *status quo* represented (and rendered intelligible) in the conspectus, in consequence of the impact exerted by the plan. Clearly, what matters is not whether the plan faithfully depicts the *status quo* and its likely "development" but on the contrary in which respects the plan deviates from reality, and to what extent it does so in each of these respects.

Development policy: creative introduction of deviations from existing trends

Here one runs once more into the difference between conspectus and plan. Since it appears in a different perspective now, its significance receives a new light. This light will prove to vindicate the long-winding argument, above, for a faithful and careful, true conspectus, rather than a simplistic preconceived one, as the only sensible base for development planning and action, including feed-back and evaluation.

The point here is that the arbitrary act that is crucial to distilling plan from conspectus is not merely an act of forcible simplification in presentation, as we had to describe it a while ago. From the present viewpoint, this same act proves to be a potentially creative act: namely in that it provides the basis for effective steering towards development.

In this light, the crucial nature of the two remarks made above becomes even more obvious. The plan must deviate from the conspectus, and this in a manner different from the way in which the conspectus will inevitably "differ from" actual reality: its inherent simplification and consistency represent conscious, maybe even purposive, human volition. Thus, the questions in which regards it will deviate, and how much, are really the crucial ones. An overdose of deviation will kill all chances of the policy based on the plan: it is senseless to fix as the economic goal for next year an increase of per capita income by 20%; and it is equally senseless to demand the effectuation at short notice of full-fledged democracy, whatever that may be. Considerations of gradualism enter again, but in a rather different sense than when we used the word above. Gradualism, to be sure, that even the staunchest revolutionary cannot evade without impunity. There is more sense to the "white" revolution of the Shah-an-Shah of Iran than some are willing to concede (but they may not know Afghan history). In the same manner, the points at which plan will deviate from conspectus are crucial: each of them should ideally represent a strategic decision, and each of them, in order to be considered significant, should make for an irreversible trend. Where there is irreversibility, slowness is no longer a main consideration.

Conclusion

In a provisional summing-up one may say that evaluation as feed-back is the permanent search for optimal impact on reality on the part of the development agent: resulting from deliberate choices as regards the respects in which development plan will deviate from conspectus of development goals and also as regards the degree of deviation. By implication, this search will take into account the interaction between development agent and development situation at large: this, after all, should be part of the implementation of planned goals.

Against the backdrop of these considerations, feed-back is in principle a permanent exercise in comparative "dynamics" (if the term is permissible), moving back and forth between reality-as-process, as rendered in the (in principle continuously modified) conspectus on the one hand, and plan on the other. In its turn, the plan, like the conspectus, will originate at one point in time but will in principle be subject to constant modification ever after. The modification will, obviously, refer both to the respects in which the plan will deviate from reality (as presented in the conspectus) and to which extent.

If this would seem to exclude any hard and fast, eternal policy lines, that would seem to be a simple matter of realism. If, on the other hand, it would seem to undermine any regularity and cumulative effect, in other words any "real development" in the common-speech sense of the term, then the plan lacks vision or the policy lacks power of conviction. Vision and conviction do count: there is no natural law that says that for such and such conditions such and such a plan is correct, and any other plan wrong.

16

CURRENT WRITINGS ON DEVELOPMENT INDICATORS

The preceding argument concerning the evaluation of development contains no explicit reference to the existing literature. Some brief references are to find a place here. Their main purpose will be further clarification of what has been attempted in the foregoing.

A terminological matter

A terminological remark must open the proceedings. The current name for that with which we are concerned is indicators of development. Indicators sounds innocent enough: it is something like barometer readings. If it proves less innocent and in many ways more difficult than it appears, this is mainly for lack of something to serve as a barometer. This problem has been discussed above and needs no repeating.

Another source of difficulty, and one that does need mention here, lies in the circumstance that in current usage the concept indicator appears to constitute a smooth transition from "symptom" to "programme point" – in other words, from the retrospective to the prospective view of development. It was already argued that this transition is by no means a simple matter. A merely verbal device that tends to make it appear smooth is therefore bound to be deceptive. Indeed, in the light of what was said above, the link between symptom of achieved development and leverage point for intended development, far from being a matter of identity or coincidence between the two, needs careful scrutiny case by case. If and when it occurs, it is likely to be in the manner in which steering and feed-back belong together: a more or less circular process (with built-in devices against becoming a vicious circle).

The implication is that a model for development policy and a model for development evaluation are not basically the same thing. Granting possible resemblance, they are fundamentally apart. And one cannot afford to overlook this difference, the way one is tempted to do when using the term indicators loosely.[1]

Limitations to present discussion

Again, this is not the occasion to discuss the strictly economic literature on indicators of development. The reasons were given above: the range developed here is purposely much wider. Some purportedly economic treatises on development do show an adequate awareness of the existence of non-economic side by side with economic factors or indicators. Thus, Rostow's study,[2] which marks the beginning of the discussion on the subject. If his listing of a handful of basic "propensities" sounds somewhat crude and primitive now, this is largely thanks to his success in prompting others to continue what he began.

For present purposes it will be useful to devote some thought to three kinds of writings in the broad field concerned. (1) One refers to the detection of crucial considerations in respect of long-range developments: a line of thought for which particularly B. de Jouvenel and his concept of *futuribles* are significant. (2) Secondly, the current fashion to analyze entire societies or states, and for this purpose to itemize them,

---

[1]   This temptation is furthered from yet another side. What has been called here, carefully, symptoms of development, is often called factors of development. The term factor connotes a world of thought and action that, as has been said before, is quite common amongst those who deal with development problems. This world is made up by unilinear causal sequences: perhaps not overtly deterministic but never quite free from determinism, perhaps not entirely based on the oversimplifications of monofactor explanation but never quite free from the urge to reduce explanatory factors to the minimum. It is a world where the given explanation for one case will necessarily be the valid recipe for the next similar case. The reason is that the act of tracing a thing back to its causal factors is, in the last resort, the detection and mastery of its essence. In having explained it, the mind dominates it. At the root of this trend of reasoning stands the postulate of solipsistic Promethean reason, as the cornerstone of the universe. Without too much explicit or systematic revolting against this pattern of thought, contemporary thinking has moved quite far away from it. However, precisely for lack of a clear break between the two, there is a risk of confusion. The mind may relapse into the older thought pattern any time it faces serious difficulties in operating the contemporary one. This temptation is particularly grave in matters of development, where one is bound to work with the unknown shape of things to come. Relapses, in cases like these, will usually involve undue reliance on given recipes or formulas. More often than not, these will – additional relapse stemming from the same difficulty – involve ethnocentrism too. A concept like factors tends to come only too handy for purposes like these. It is, therefore, well to point out that, crucial as the concept factors was to 19th century Western thought with its causal, more or less mechanistic, explanation, it is virtually useless in the framework of contemporary thinking.
[2]   W. W. Rostow, *The Process of Economic Growth* (Oxford, Clarendon, 1953).

whether quantifyingly or otherwise. The fashionable name is "systems". As a line of thought this does not appear too different, fundamentally, from input-output analysis *à la* Leontieff in economics. (3) The third, and the only one in this list referring to development in the strict sense, is the attempt to list, broadly yet consistently, the indicators that together should provide a manageable tool whether for policy or for evaluation.

"Futuribles"

To read the future has always been a profoundly human need. It is one expression of the need to realize that life makes sense, even if unknown. Ever since, in Western society, the magician has been abolished and the priest has abstained from the task, the historian has had a special vocation to concern himself with the future. This has not completely changed since, rather recently, the perception of reality that brought the Western brand of history writing to the fore has changed once again, and in so doing has demolished some of the grounds for the historian's prerogative in this regard. Planners may have taken over part of what historians used to do in regard to the future, but not nearly all. One could even doubt whether Flechtheim and his reviewer Cazes [3] are correct in agreeing, more or less, that if the shorter range belongs to the planner, the longer still belongs to the historian. This would seem to be largely a matter of further considerations involved.

One of these refers necessarily to the link between past and future, an old historians' concern. The other refers to the nature and clarity of available indicators. Flechtheim has some things to say on either point.

In arguing why, particularly now, historians should – and should be able to – consider the future besides the past he uses two arguments. One is, the fast developments occurring in the present. The other is, the improvement of scientific instruments for forecasting future developments. With futurology thus claimed to be possible, he proceeds to surround the discussion of its nature with ample caution. No claim is made that man could mould the future. It is merely a matter of effectuating some modification or perhaps of seeking some degree of protection from what seems to be in store. This conception is not too far apart from what has been argued above in respect of tendencies towards development. On the other hand, the argument does not appear quite

[3] Ossip K. Flechtheim, *History and Futurology* (Meisenheim, Hain, 1966). Review essay by B. Cazes, in *History and Theory*, VI/3 (Middletown, Conn., Wesleyan, 1967), pp. 436-450.

satisfactory so far as the link between retrospective and prospective approaches are concerned. Cazes, in his review, tries to improve the first point somewhat by adding accumulation to acceleration. Even so, the hard core of the problem has not been reached. In this respect, therefore, the matter discussed above is underscored but not brought any further.

Turning now to areas or sectors where one may look for indications of future developments, Cazes has attempted to provide a brief listing of Flechtheim's suggestions. Summarizing a summary, they can be listed as follows,

(1) personal anticipation of events in life, with or without expert assistance;
(2) "nature", *e.g.*, climate, human longevity;
(3) technological innovations;
(4) demographic and economic forecasting;
(5) national political development;
(6) international trends;
(7) future developments of (Western) civilization.

Upon closer inspection, this list proves extremely complex, and for this reason somewhat elusive. It distinguishes the individual realm (1) from the supra-individual (2-7). It distinguishes the "natural" (2) from the man-made human context (3), and those together from some rest (4-7). It distinguishes more or less statistical (4) from more or less intuitive (5-7) ways of forecasting. Amongst the latter, it distinguishes the specifically cultural (7) from the more or less political (5, 6). And within the political, it distinguishes the national or internal (5) from the international (6). Together, these distinctions, overly systematized for present purposes, could hardly add up to one consistent scheme. As a classificatory scheme, Flechtheim's approach, even in Cazes's systematic rendering, is disappointing. Consequently, it cannot be hoped to be effective as a base line for purposes of identifying clues for future developments. The reason for this failure may well be the lack of consideration of necessary underlying principles of systematization. Once again, the conclusion seems to be that the importance of a point argued above is underscored, without the point itself being brought any further than where it was carried in the preceding.

"Social accounting"
In choosing Bertram M. Gross's model of analysis of total societies, one

runs into the question, not unusual since systems became fashionable, whether a nation is a kind of system or alternatively a system is the abstracting expansion of something commonly called a nation: the expansion aiming at inclusion of any nations and any units not called nations.[4]

The approach is said to constitute ultimately "an instrument of prediction and control" (Gross p. 3): thus implicitly postulating an identity of two approaches distinguished above, the prospective and the retrospective. If this could become a problem, it remains largely academic. The claim is immediately withdrawn and replaced by a statement of intention that does not go beyond description and explanation. This sounds like a withdrawal from new but frightening territory to the safe ground of established thought patterns: unfortunately without explicit vindication of their tenability today.

With due regard for plurality and complexity, systems are dealt with from the viewpoint of one who is to assess them (p. 1), both essentially (structure) and operationally (performance). This combination recalls structural-functionalism and the philosophical tradition of earlier days; it is introduced without argument as to its applicability, as a more or less self-evident first step. Taking its clue from economic accounting, the attempt is to expand the accounting approach, so as to render it comprehensive in respect of the system concerned (p. 15ff). That this could be, or perhaps is in effect bound to be, to a large extent a matter of definitions is not discussed in so many words.

The result of this effort is a descriptive blueprint, a set of pegs on which to hang things. It comes in two parts, one for system structure and one for system performance. Structure is said (p. 39, 46f) to consist of (a) people, (b) non-human resources, (c) subsystems, (d) internal relations, (e) external relations, (f) values and (g) central guidance system. In similar fashion, performance is broken down (p. 41, 84f) into (a) satisfying interests, (b) producing output, (c) investing in system, (d) using output efficiently, (e) acquiring resources, (f) observing codes and (g) behaving rationally. That the two sets have the same number of items seems to be a coincidence. In the second set, the impact of

[4] B. M. Gross, *The State of the Nation, o.c.* (above, Ch. 3, nt. 8). Comp. Raymond A. Bauer, *Social Indicators* (Cambridge, Mass., M.I.T., 1966). See also A. S. Banks and R. Textor, *A Cross-Polity Survey* (Cambridge, Mass., M.I.T., 1963); R. L. Merritt and S. Rokkan (eds.), *Comparing Nations, The Use of Quantitative Data in Cross-National Research* (New Haven, Yale, 1966); B. M. Russett, H. R. Alker, Jr., K. W. Deutsch and H. D. Lasswell, *World Handbook of Political and Social Indicators* (New Haven, Yale U.P., 1964).

economic thought, including the classical rationality tenet, is quite visible. In fact, the main distinctive feature of the scheme as compared to customary economics seems to be the rather more metaphorical use of standard terminology.

The inner systematics in either case is largely a matter of addition of considerations of various kinds (p. 38f). Consequently it would seem to elude further analysis. Nor is this matter very important: the pegs serve to hang virtually anything. Each of them is said to be multidimensional (p. 39) and the elaboration to which they lend themselves is so catholic as to allow incorporation of a good deal of Parsonian pattern variables (p. 67f) and Kluckhohnian dichotomies (p. 68ff). In consequence, the apparatus offered, whether for descriptive or other purposes, is essentially a catch-all device. Given the intent to secure a grip on reality the effort made thus begins to appear as self-defeating.

Similar doubts arise in another respect. The dichotomy of structure and performance inevitably connotes the traditional distinction between statics and dynamics. But it is not the only way in which change is made to feature in the scheme. At one point, conflict is given its due as a source of change (p. 30). More attention goes to a kind of comparative statics of a largely typological nature (quoting Lerner and others). Interestingly, it is applied to both structure and performance. It runs between pre-industrial, industrial and post-industrial systems (p. 78ff, 129ff). As is often the case, the elaboration remains conceptual. Its actual relevance to any given real situation would depend, to a considerable extent, on a good deal of inductive work that would have to be undertaken starting out from that situation and virtually regardless of the scheme. Thus the intended comprehensiveness of the model is at odds with its exclusive reliance on the deductive approach.

The occurrence of this difficulty could well signal a more deeply rooted problem. This problem, it would seem, centres around the very concept of system. As a catch-all device, it is the product of a particular kind of abstracting generalization. It is generalization and abstraction in response to the natural urge to get away from the observed and inventorized concrete situation of which the observer himself is part, namely by evading the limitations attributed to its specificity. In other words, generalization by means of demolition of specificity. Here is a profound and fundamental question, that perhaps lies at the root of a good deal of systems theory, but that is not dealt with in the study now under review. And rightly, so: it had to be presupposed. Unfortunately, what the book does give seems to indicate that one could not really

afford to assume that this basic question had been dealt with satisfactorily. Once system has been defined in a manner so as to disregard
specificity rather than to account for it, it becomes a catch-all device
that is necessarily at odds with the stated goals of Professor Gross's
effort, namely to be useful towards providing (a) structure information,
(b) means for goal formulation, (c) means for evaluation (p. 12). The
conclusion appears as an argument in favour of two signal features by
which the preceding discussion differs from the Gross model, namely
selectivity and the consistent effort to account for specificity of sociocultural entities. Social systems are not just complexes, they are meaningful complexes (and meaningful is not the same as rational).

"Levels of living"

The various reports on levels of living belong in the atmosphere of
action and related thought where development is by and large conceived as improved satisfaction of needs.[5] Typically, it is the atmosphere

---

[5]   Jan Drewnowski and Wolf Scott, *The Level of Living Index* (Geneva, [UN-
RISD Report 4] 1966), mimeo. Comp. *Report on International Definition and
Measurement of Standards and Levels of Living* (New York, [UN, E/CN.3/179,
E/CN.5/299], 1954), mimeo; *International Definition and Measurement of Levels
of Living, An Interim Guide* (UN, E/CN.2/270/Rev.1, E/CN.5/353), 1961
(mimeo); N. Baster and M. Subramanian, *Aspects of Social and Economic
Growth* (Geneva [UNRISD Report 1], 1965), mimeo; Jan Drewnowski, *Social
and Economic Factors in Development* (Geneva [UNRISD Report 3], 1966),
mimeo. See also C. J. L. Bertholet and B. H. Evers, *Measuring Socio-Economic
Development, A Pilot Study* (Tilburg, Inst. f. Dev. Probl., 1965), mimeo, restricted; B. Evers, "Arm en rijk", *Maandschrift Economie*, 31/2 (Tilburg, 1966),
pp. 81-97.
   In this connection mention may also be made of a recent report referring to the
evaluation of development aid projects: *Methods and Procedures of Evaluation
in Development Aid*, Conference Report, German Foundation for Developing
Countries (Berlin, November 1966), mimeo, Dok. 352 IT23/66, with bibliography.
Although the evaluation of development aid projects belongs within the broader
range of what is being discussed here, it is a much more restricted proposition
and one that naturally tends to maintain its inherent limitations. In the framework of a given development process, an aid project can necessarily constitute no
more than one out of a multiplicity of factors and forces. Moreover – let us face
it – there is no compelling reason why it should be a preponderant factor or
force. The consequence is that in assessing the efficacy of an aid project one
may be doing anything but keeping one's finger on the pulse of development
proper. Even more important is that to widen one's vision from an aid project
with which one is involved towards the development process concerned as a whole
is particularly difficult. In identifying with an aid project one is bound to assume
it to be if not the gravitation point at least the main leverage point of the development process concerned. The full complexity of the latter may, therefore, prove
at odds with the approach one develops towards it. Stretching the argument a bit

of U.N. and affiliated agencies: but it tends to reappear in many other variants of development action.

The concept of needs is crucial. Most people are aware that needs are culture-conditioned and are prepared to pay lip service to the fact. There are many, however, whom this does not prevent from proceeding right away towards the establishment of "general" human needs. From this postulate to an aprioristic listing of needs is a simple step, and not really a difficult one, given a healthy dose of ethnocentrism.

From listing needs to using the list for development purposes, whether policy making or evaluation, is a less simple step, but it should be well worth trying. One or two problems need to be solved on the way. Thus, the too narrowly economic concern with development, as expressed, amongst other things, in a too narrowly economic definition of needs, should be remedied by expansion or addition: a point also argued by Gross. This allows the introduction of the concept social in addition, and perhaps as a corrective, to the concept economic. The question remains, however, whether it will allow broadening of the focus to such an extent as to effectively scan development in all its length and width.

Another problem is the cumulative significance of all the needs that one may have distinguished and listed. This is not the same as the problem, discussed above, of the inner systematics of a list. In most reports here under review, that matter has been attended to quite satisfactorily. The question here is whether all listed needs together make up a picture of wanted development, and accordingly whether a list of their satisfaction is a picture of achieved development. The sharp edge of this question is usually blurred in the manner already discussed in connection with Gross's shift from prognostication and evaluation to description: data on need satisfaction are primarily used for purposes of comparing existing situations in various countries or areas. They are not directly used as clues for goal identification or as yardsticks for evaluation. Insofar as they will be made to serve for such purposes, this will happen in the indirect way, using discrepancies or similarities observed through comparison.

The same blurring is further enhanced by the fact that comparability can nowadays be achieved in one way only, namely through quantification. Whether a particular indicator will be attributed all the significance that one would expect it to have will depend, to a perhaps un-

---

beyond its present focus, one arrives here at the verity that a development aid viewpoint could well be a drawback rather than an asset if it comes to developing a way of dealing adequately with phenomena of development.

pleasantly large extent, on its quantifiability. Weighing – a problem in itself, no doubt – may remedy this partially, but doubts remain. At any rate, the consequence is that henceforth the matter is by and large a statistician's problem.

Returning to the hard core issues, it appears worth pointing out that the word social could become misleading. There is no clear difference between someone's social and his economic needs.[6] Indeed, there is reason to suspect that the addition of social to economic needs is basically nothing but the necessary widening of a conception that had for some time been used in an unrealistically narrow definition: definition to be sure, that had been made by a past generation of social scientists who happened to be known as economists.

The hard core problem in the connection may not be the addition of social to economic needs, whether as a corrective or merely for completeness's sake. Rather, it refers to the conception of development that pivots on need satisfaction. Any concept of this kind operates on a reductionist basis. It assumes that any sociocultural entity, whether person, group or nation, is adequately represented as individual human being(s) and, secondly, that this individual human being, the atom of society, is adequately represented as the incorporation of needs. *Homo indigens*.

The U.N. committee of experts must have realized this and attempted a corrective without seeming to go beyond the confines of their brief. Some of the "basic information" they desire refers in fact to other aspects of sociocultural reality than *homo indigens*. So do some of the traditional economic items that creep into lists here and there. The crucial point seems to be that if development is social, it must necessarily be societal as well. This, however, is a consideration for which hardly any room can be made in a conception that takes development to be, by and large, improved need satisfaction. If room is made, the term need must acquire wider and in fact different meaning and become synonymous to terms used in the preceding, such as tendencies, or, slightly narrower, needs in the still very broad sense in which the word was employed in the scheme concerning clues for the identification of goals.

---

[6] It is perhaps interesting to see some similarities and differences in existing choices in regard to indicators of levels of need satisfaction. Left column, UN Committee of Experts on the International Definition and Measurement of Standards and Levels of Living, report 1954 as summarized 1961. Middle column, Drewnowski and Scott, UNRISD report 4, 1966. Right column, Bertholet and

All this amounts to saying that in the scheme developed on p. 66 the approach of these reports belongs at the purely deductive end, where general theoretical indications are listed. Whilst broadening the scope it remains a partial approach, and its accordingly limited nature is something that should not be overlooked.

Evers, as summarized in Dutch by Evers (p. 100 of quoted article). The latter differs from the other two in that it shows economic considerations explicitly whereas the others presuppose them tacitly.

(I-Components of Levels of Living)	(I-Basic Needs)	
	(A-Physical)	
2. food cons. and nutrition	1. nutrition	II. nutrition
5. housing	2. shelter	—
7. clothing		
1. health	3. health	I. health
	(B-Cultural)	
3. education	4. education	III. education
8. education	5. leisure, recreation	—
6. soc. security		
9. human freedoms	6. security	—
	(II-Additional Needs)	
—	7. surplus income	VIII. savings, investment, cap. product., econ. growth
4. employment and cond. of work	—	VII. econ. structure
—	—	V. urbanization
—	—	IX. internal market
—	—	X. foreign commerce
—	—	XI. "monoculture"
(II-Basic Inform.)		
1. population and labour force	—	XII. demogr. variables
2. income and expend.	—	VI. income
3. communications and transportation		
a. mass	—	IV. mass communication
b. post & tele	—	
c. transportation	—	

PART IV

COMPLICATIONS

17

THE COLD WAR

The understanding of development may also be furthered by exposing some undue image-formation. There are certain images currently in use and certain much-discussed distracting issues that deserve some critical attention lest they thwart the proper understanding of development. As an example of distracting issues one may quote the cold war; one example of incorrect image formation is the metaphor of the class struggle.

The cold war is an ominous case in point showing the already mentioned need for a new system of world relationships. The colonial-imperial order is gone. Two powers, of greater magnitude than the ones that used to control the Western empires, and not hitherto fully effective in the framework of international affairs, have found themselves irrevocably part of the world scene. It is not likely that such involvement was fully intended from the outset (that is, from the moment when they joined World War II) by those concerned. One assumes that the inclination must have been to persist in a relatively undisturbed existence as universes by themselves. The parallel fates of the Russian "Westerners" and of people like Wilson in the U.S. seem to demonstrate that tendencies towards more effective involvement in the world did occur in either country but were by and large ineffective. However, what they could not achieve has been brought about in the aftermath of the war. The two powers are definitely part of the world scene.

Yet neither of them, upon entering it, was ready or capable to shed the self-view of uniqueness that comes with being a universe in your own right: the self-view that, as was argued before, appears most significantly as ethnocentrism. In consequence, either power entered the world with claims to leadership backed up by the conviction that what is good for "us" is good for the world. The immediate consequence is that they are fully competitive. This is further dramatized in the creation of the new world order insofar as this occurs through the creation of new members of that order. The urge to put new nations on their feet has at times taken on the appearance of competitive proliferation, each super-power being intent to spawn faithful replicas of itself with which, in observance of the Old Testament commandment, to fill the world.

Ideology as an element in image formation

Note that all this has nothing whatsoever to do with the respective ideologies, even though, under the circumstances, these tend to feature as competing orthodoxies. The ideologies enter as *post facto* rationaliza-tions: neither more nor less. This helps to explain the intriguing varia-bility of interpretation of terms like communist in U.S. usage and, in U.S.S.R. usage, of terms like imperialist and colonialist. Terms like these fulfil the same function as the term *barbaros* in classical Greek: they make it possible to detractingly account for a disturbance in the image that a given society has of its universe, – disturbance caused by some entity the presence of which makes no sense. Another good ex-ample in the connection is "behind the Iron Curtain".

It is perhaps good to underscore that in relating the creation of new nations to the urge to reorganize the world, my attempt was not to achieve some literary effect. The two are vitally related. But they are essentially vitiated by the competition involved, which is a carry-over from an obsolete state of affairs. And speaking of carry-over: the nation-state, which is immediately involved, originates in the West-European climate rather than in either the U.S. or the U.S.S.R. This inevitably makes the matter even more problematic.

Regardless now of these fundamental considerations, the practice of some twenty years seems to indicate that to divide the world into two competing halves is just not feasible. Unfortunately, the main occur-rences supporting this conclusion have meant nothing towards the necessary clarification of the basic issue. Neither the emergence of powerless neutralism, amorphous as it was, nor that of a third super-power, in many respects virtual rather than actual,[1] have really affected

---

[1]   Insofar as the Chinese stand is clear it would seem to differ, for the time being, from both that of the USSR and that of the US, but perhaps in degree rather than in principle. The vital issue, as argued, is the manner in which a given society (that is, a given sociocultural entity complete with its own uni-verse) will account for the realization that in the actual world of geography and of communications unlimited, states, nations and what not exist that are decidedly not part of that given society's universe. How will the self-view accommodate that by which it is disturbingly affected? Now one could perhaps argue that to the USA, ethnocentrism is saved by toning it down in two ways that reinforce one another mutually. One, the world at large is seen to feature as a more or less natural extension to self, rather than, according to the traditional view, a disturb-

world relationships as a pattern. They merely add to the problem that remains unresolved and by and large untackled: the problem of how to envisage the role of ethnocentrism, as a natural corollary to the existence of any sociocultural entity, in a context of effective world-wide interdependence of plural sociocultural entities. How to turn plurinational chaos into international cosmos?

Cold war and development aid

Considered in this light, the mix-up of cold war and international assistance is more than an undesirable and useless complication. To give an example. It could seem only proper if two agencies of the type of CIA on the one hand and AID on the other should use entirely different, almost contrary norms in their respective activities. But this cannot be. Both in the field and at home, each will inevitably account for the other, and to an extent perhaps adjust to its existence, in goal setting as well as in application of means. Strictly speaking, it will thereby necessarily distort its own, and perhaps also the other's, operational pattern. The confusion-in-principle that thus comes into existence is bad at the "giving" end but it is perhaps even worse at the receiving end. It is perhaps mainly due to confusions like these that for example the allegiance of Pakistan to the West has swerved in a manner that has for some time been quite bewildering to certain Westerners. It is, no doubt, the same confusion that prompts the more imaginative leaders of certain

---

ance inflicted upon the universe constituted by and around self. In the perspective of American history, this shift appears quite natural and feasible: by and large, Americans originate consciously from elsewhere in the world. Two, alien societies are consequently envisaged as affiliated to self. But the term affiliation is avoided: bad conscience about ethnocentrism dictates the use of euphemisms such as friendship and co-operation. (With the added advantage that thus a way opens up to a further, and more effective, toning down of ethnocentrism.)

To China, ethnocentrism seems for the time being to offer less cause for uneasiness. Insofar as the outside world would have to be envisaged in anything like an effective relationship with China, that is, the Chinese universe, the only way to achieve this would be by becoming China's shadow: by conforming. But even such conformity could not result in the Chinese universe becoming effectively extended so as to comprise the whole world. If this could be a more or less correct rendering of what appears to be the Chinese position, then one should be entitled to expect more or less significant modifications in the course of time, in case the Chinese isolation were to diminish.

As regards the USSR, its position would seem to waver in between the two just sketched. On the one hand there is a trend to lean over to the variant here described for the USA. On the other hand there could be some cool policy calculation behind a protracted wavering, since this should provide a useful tool in the competition against the USA.

developing nations to cajole ever new aid for ever new purposes out of advanced nations on either side of the Iron Curtain.

It could thus appear as if in today's international world nothing could be more desirable than to disentangle cold war from international assistance. At the same time, however, one realizes that nothing could be less feasible. What is not always followed through is the realization that even if complete disentangling is out of the question, distinguishing might do some good. The point is that, as was already argued, both the cold war and the problem of development (particularly in its implication of development assistance) are symptoms, and equally important ones, of the changes actually taking place in the world constellation. One could argue that whereas the cold war signals these changes mainly with respect to the interaction between optimal sociocultural entities (commonly called nation-states), development signals the same: but primarily with respect to the self-realization, the operational crystallization, of each of these separately. Thus considered, the two constitute a clear mutuality of perspective. Again, there would seem to be occasion for applying, to either order of problems, the same basic understanding of development as a variant of process. If only one could have at one's disposal the adequate elaboration of general development theory that would apply, on the one hand, to the development of particular sociocultural entities and, on the other, to the mutual interaction of several sociocultural entities each going through development, then the present mix-up between cold war and international assistance would be reduced to the status of a subsequent and subsidiary problem: namely, how to conceive of the interconnections between these two aspects of one and the same world-wide process. This would still not be an easy matter to cope with, but at least it could no longer present insuperable difficulties in principle.

Overzealous interpretations of conflict

Two further difficulties must also be mentioned at this point. One is that when sociologists, political scientists and even politicians deal with the problem of "international" relations, they will tend to conceive it in terms of conflict, whether actual or potential. Besides, the notion of conflict that they employ for the purpose will show the Western bent of mind: the urge towards (creative) conflict resolution, whether by elimination of the subject matter of conflict or by elimination of the opponent. Now it is undeniable that once ethnocentrism–competition–conflict are assumed to form an unbreakable sequence, this is the only way to deal with the phenomenon: *si vis pacem para bellum* – if you desire peace be ready for war. There is some logic to the arms race. On the other hand, it has not been proven that no alternative logical sequence is available. And since the world can no longer afford war, having virtually eliminated the creative outcome of all-out conflict, there would seem to be occasion – in fact, there is an urgent need – to reconsider this sequence in a purposeful attempt to determine where it goes wrong.[2]

Theoretically speaking, this signals the dire need for a fundamental overhaul in basic conceptualization. If we envisage conflict differently than we do now, we are bound to envisage its potential implications differently and in consequence we could find our behaviour channelled along lines of different self-fulfilling prophecies.

Practically speaking, it underscores the need, already signalled, for a novel frame of reference – one that would apply to big-power relationships equally much as to development policies as to international relations in general. Unfortunately, this conclusion sounds like a well-worn platitude. That, however, is no good reason for shrugging it off, as too many are inclined to do. Again, if there exists a general tendency to shy away from the problem, it should be worth determining what holds people back.

---

[2] On a different perception of conflict and one that is in a sense less value loaded, comp. my "The Tribal Sector in Middle Eastern Society: A Profile", *o.c.*

18

HAVES AND HAVE-NOTS

Much the same line of argument applies it it comes to proving that in matters of developed versus developing countries, the class struggle cannot serve as a paradigm because it is obsolete. Intriguingly, this is one thought model that is used both by people "in the free world" and by people "behind the Iron Curtain", – with the difference, however, that whilst the latter give it a tinge of zeal, the former tend to make it sound gloomy. But if these devices are calculated to make the haves – have-nots model more effective, they surely do not remedy its falseness, its being a hollow piece of rhetoric.

The criterion of material wealth: a case of reductionism

For one thing, the material wealth criterion [1] neglects and virtually falsifies the comprehensiveness of the change-development process. Then, statistical averages for countries have disconcertingly little to do with cohesions or solidarities within countries concerned, and hardly more with solidarities between countries: take Africa, take the Middle East. This is not to deny the existence of the Widening Gap, or its importance; but it is to maintain that the haves – have-nots dichotomy is an unfit conceptual means to refer to it. The Marxian construct, even if it did apply to England during the Industrial Revolution, does not necessarily lend itself to infinite expansion through metaphorical use: not from class to state, not from one period to another, not from one culture context to another. Any time these limitations are overlooked, its expanded use threatens to turn it into a scarecrow, a stumbling block for both thought and action.

[1] Comp. L. J. Zimmerman, *Arme en rijke landen, Een economische analyse*, 2e dr. (Den Haag, Albani, 1964).

PART V

IMPLICATIONS FOR SOCIAL SCIENCES THEORY AND TEACHING

19

INTRODUCTION

Thus far, the various ways in which the concept of development has been modified during two decades have been discussed largely for their own sake. Implications have been suggested here and there, mostly without distinguishing between implications for theory and implications for action. There is nothing against this insofar as the two are necessarily interrelated anyway.

Even so, it appears useful to spell out in some more detail a few of the implications of what was said thus far for the dealings that social scientists have with matters of development. It appears that these implications are nothing short of revolutionizing. In taking the matter up under four headings, I shall have occasion to elaborate certain observations already made in passing. The headings are, (1) the nature of change, (2) interdisciplinary integration, (3) the replacement of objectification by mutual relevance for purposes of interaction, (4) education for development.

20

CHANGE

First, the matter of change. Like major social philosophies before them, the social sciences have had their formative period under conditions of change. Social philosophers and social scientists working under such conditions are likely to show an awareness as to their condition, and to work in response thereto.

Plato, in seeking to establish the principle of justice, employed the Socratic manner, thus underscoring that he and his contemporaries had little use for inherited modes of thought and action. Even so, his concern was to lay down a firm – and that is likely to mean, persistent – guide line for the present and the future. Marx was quite outspoken on the matter. His 11th thesis on Feuerbach states that whereas the philosophers have disputed about reality, what matters now is to alter it.[1] And one is inclined to conclude, from the Marxist elaboration of Marxian doctrine if not from Marx himself, that he or at least the Marxists have deviated from Hegel's precepts precisely in not being concerned about the persistence of changes to be achieved by the revolution they were (curious variant of self-fulfilling prophecy) postulating and fomenting all at once. In fact, it is the easy assumption as to the persistence of change to be brought about by revolution, that constitutes the Achilles heel of Marxism, as doctrine and as practice. But one can see, upon some further reflection, that this weakness need not be the exclusive privilege of Marxism. This point is brought out, somewhat over-dramatically, by Dahrendorf, who sees current sociology to an extent as a conservative ideology.[2] Even so, his appears to be a more correct way to envisage the matter than what has recently been propounded by

[1] Die Philosophen haben die Welt nur verschieden interpretiert, es kommt drauf an, sie zu verändern. (1845) Quoted in Iring Fetscher, *Der Marxismus, Seine Geschichte in Dokumenten, I* (München, Piper, 1962), p. 150.
[2] Ralf Dahrendorf, *Gesellschaft und Freiheit, Zur soziologischen Analyse der Gegenwart* (München, Piper, 1962), pp. 25, 47, 104.

Park,[3] who believed in a manifest function of sociology, which is the scientific study of society, and a latent function, which is obfuscation of social relations. This, it appears, is carrying Merton *ad absurdum*. Park seems to overlook the time dimension as a crucial element in the matter at hand (the common sin in a good deal of established sociology). Once this dimension is taken into account, it turns out that what we are considering is the case of the perfectly normal phenomenon of obsolescence. The validity of human ideas about human society has definite limits both in time and place.

Need for new conceptualization as regards change

Social philosophers and social scientists, like their forebears who created myths or wrote theology,[4] could be said to be engaged in altering that which, borrowing and expanding Kuhn's [5] term, one could call a paradigm. They perform the innovative function, in the rather special sense in which the term was defined a while ago: selectively bringing out one (or some) of the potentialities inherent in a prevailing state of affairs and, in so doing, affecting that state of affairs in a manner that will be perceptible as change, perhaps change with a particular direction: development. Now this function has two appearances, according to whether one perceives it retrospectively or prospectively. Prospectively, it is the effort to render a puzzling reality intelligible. Retrospectively, it

[3]   Peter Park, "The Cretan Dictum: A Functional Analysis of Sociology", *The American Sociologist*, 2/3 (Aug. 1967), pp. 155-157.
[4]   The addition of myth-makers (generations rather than persons) and theologians (schools rather than persons), not quite jokingly made, gives occasion for an important clarification. It is obvious that the argument developed in the text, in the phrasing employed, is typically and exclusively Western, if considered from the viewpoint of its acceptability. In any non-Western context where knowledge (*i.e.*, the model of the universe as interiorized in the minds of humans, usually an elite) is the treasure of the ages, eternal in nature, merely to be preserved by the living generation (and perhaps, in ritual, to be faithfully employed towards the maintenance, i.e. continued creation, of the universe), – this kind of reasoning is necessarily sacrilegious. Whilst fully accepting this verdict, one feels entitled to believe that, particularly in regard to the long run, it may be valid nevertheless. Even the doctrine of Islam, outspoken as it is on this point, does contain an (allegedly Zoroastrian) element referring to the intermittent nature, befitting time and place, of prophecy as revelation of eternal truth. Where non-West and West are decidedly different is the matter of attitude, towards shifts in doctrine and towards change in general.
[5]   Thomas S. Kuhn, *The Structure of Scientific Revolutions* (Chicago, U.P., 1962). Others use roughly the same concept with a different label; comp. for example K. E. Boulding, *The Image* (Ann Arbor, Michigan U.P., 1956). Comp. further Norwood R. Hanson, *Patterns of Discovery, An Inquiry into the Conceptual Foundations of Science* (London, Cambridge U.P., 1958).

will appear as confirmation, and, in the long run, vindication of the same reality, which in its turn will have become less puzzling and more of an existing state of affairs.

This being so, it should be considered perfectly normal that, time and again in the course of history, an existing and fairly well established body of theory turns out to have lost its relevance, to become increasingly unsatisfactory. Marx's outcry against the speculating philosophers marks such a turning point. So, perhaps, does Dahrendorf's mild accusation that sociology has become conservative ideology. In fact, this phenomenon is by no means peculiar to social philosophy and the social sciences. Kuhn has said important things about it in regard to science. Insofar as it is peculiar, it is peculiar to Western thought: and what is then peculiar is not its occurrence but a (limited) measure of readiness to accept it.

Now this is the proper perspective in which to envisage my contention that the emergence of the development problem is bound to have a revolutionizing effect on the social sciences. The current preoccupation with development is, in the last resort, a symptom of an overall change in the universe: that is, a change, affecting both our own culture universe and, inasmuch as it effectively involves this planet as a whole, everybody else's cultural universes at the same time.

Responses to need for reorientation

We (whether "we" as Western scholars or "we" as tomorrow's world citizens) face a need for all-out reorientation, more specifically a need for the creation – conceptual, intellectual and in terms of action – of a new, hopefully world-wide universe.

Insofar as social scientists, and in particular sociologists, reflect this need in their work and respond to it, they are likely to show, first, a good deal of confusion and disorientation and, subsequently, a tendency to converge upon certain ideas that thus will become at once more prominent and more articulate. A major element in this process is bound to be a shift away from reasoning in terms of timeless-and-placeless, qualitative categories, towards reasoning in terms of process, that is, of operational categories in which generality will somehow be matched, by means of inherent conceptual complementarity, with relevance to spatiotemporal and qualitative specificity.

Two of the major urges on this direction will continue to be the need to deal with change and the need to render theory operationally effective. In regard to the latter, cybernetics has shown a way that needs to be followed through.[6] In regard to the former, the real breakthrough may have to await the development of conceptual models that whilst lending themselves to mathematical presentation would not have to depend on that most desperate of all scholarly techniques, quantification.

[6] Norbert Wiener, *The Human Use of Human Beings, Cybernetics and Society* (Garden City, N.Y., Doubleday [Anchor], 1954). Comp. *idem, Cybernetics, Or Control and Communication in the Animal and the Machine* (New York, Wiley, 1948).

21

INTERDISCIPLINARY INTEGRATION

If conceptualization in terms of process is one characteristic element of today's revolutionary developments in the social sciences, interdisciplinary integration will necessarily be another. The point was mentioned above. Once reality, as instanced in any specific entities, is envisaged in terms of process – of which change and development are mere variants –, it follows necessarily that the effort to render it intelligible could hardly be considered adequate if eclectically restricted to one or, for that matter, several detached morsels thereof.

The mind vis-à-vis the comprehensiveness of reality

No doubt, this raises the thorny issue of the mind's dealings with comprehensiveness as one characteristic of reality. The cause of the difficulty would seem to be that the mind's operational pattern is the opposite of comprehensive.[1] Mental "comprehension" (the term is perfectly wrong)

---

[1] Suzanne K. Langer, *Philosophical Sketches* (Baltimore, Johns Hopkins, 1962). Further elaboration in *idem, Mind, An Essay on Human Feeling*, Vol. I (Baltimore, Johns Hopkins, 1967); further vols. to appear. This work, of which at the time of this writing only Vol. I is available, provides first of all some penetrating criticisms of certain fashionable trends in the social sciences (Ch. 2). They are mostly aimed at psychology, but sociologists and economists had better not believe themselves invulnerable to the philosopher's arrows. The presentation and conceptualization of reality presented in Pt. III employ a different terminology than has been adopted for the present essay; but the parallels are striking and encouraging. Central to Dr. Langer's conceptualization is the concept of the act (not to be confused with current sociological use of the term action). For one of its aspects, namely if taken in the sense in which it expands into "evolution of acts", this concept seems to run parallel to the concept of emergence as used here. For the other of its aspects, namely the sense in which it expands into agent, it seems to parallel the concept of sociocultural entity as used here. This is perhaps the occasion to underscore the fundamental relatedness and virtual identity of the two concepts employed in this essay. This is of course better indicated in Dr. Langer's one term than by the use of two terms; even so I find it more convenient to use this pair of terms rather than just one embracing term. Furthermore, the matter discussed by Dr. Langer as individuation and involvement,

is achieved by dividing and delimiting, by analysis in the strict sense of the word. Analysis, moreover, is usually carried out in the assumption that there is no reason to bother about reconstitution. This may be on account of the scanning that is the typical operational complement of all the dividing and delimiting that the mind undertakes. Although it is not reconstituting, and in fact never could take its place, it clearly does serve as a viable substitute for all practical purposes. The categories or morsels into which the mind has abstractingly and objectifyingly analyzed reality are assumed to prove recomposed into the fullness of reality at any desired moment.

Yet this very assumption causes trouble when applied to the matter of distinct disciplines in the social sciences versus comprehensiveness of sociocultural reality. The reason is, quite simply, that in this case things do not work out as they should. Of course, it is possible to bring together social scientists of various disciplines in order that they engage in some interdisciplinary project. Too often, however, the result is confusion or paralysis rather than smoothly running comprehensiveness. This state of affairs clearly and recognizedly constitutes a problem. It is the more serious inasmuch as anyone identified with any particular discipline disqualifies for purposes of trying his hand at its solution. Those of the other disciplines are bound to expect that he will succumb to some kind of solipsism in favour of his discipline, parallelling the solipsism of groups or nations commonly called ethnocentrism.

The entrenchment of disciplines

Indeed there can be no doubt that disciplines are not simply, as the name says, specializations by subject matter and by method to deal therewith. Besides, they lead a life as groups or factions, – in other words, as sociocultural entities complete with their own self-identification and ensuing (view of the) universe.

---

again two complementary aspects of basically one phenomenon (but this time she too uses two terms), go here by different yet closely parellel names, namely identity and context (or frame of reference).

The circumstance that Dr. Langer aims at a comprehensive view of reality, not philosophical in any narrow sense but indeed stretching into biology and science on the one hand and into creative art on the other, renders these parallelisms the more important for present purposes. A parochial sociology entrenched in a narrow technical vision of its object will warrant less hope that it will prove significant for society than a sociology that partakes in a fuller, more comprehensive view of reality.

Comp. also Jean-Paul Sartre, *Critique de la raison dialectique*, t. 1 (Paris, Gallimard, 1960).

This being so, it seems worth probing deeper in order to ascertain which factors, besides professional associations and organizational convenience in educational institutions, may have induced this development. Turning to the history of ideas, one finds considerable enlightenment in works like Gusdorf's,[2] in which particular attention is paid to the differentiation of disciplines that was the corollary to the mushrooming of the social sciences. What really matters, of course, is the modalities of this differentiation and the conditions prompting it.

The far-reaching implications of objectification

Anticipating a good deal of work that remains to be done on the subject, and under proviso of possible correction, one is inclined to point an accusing finger, once more, towards objectification as a dominant characteristic of early social sciences thought. Once objectification is granted as a valid way to deal with reality, reality in its turn is virtual object to the human mind, or more precisely: reality is modifiable, relative object to mind as given, absolute subject. In consequence, it is only logical to maintain furthermore that segmentation, applied by the mind in regard to its object, reality, is the appropriate manner of coping with that object's comprehensiveness. After all, this merely means drawing the consequence from the subject-object dichotomy as the basic segmentation.

What remains to be said about all this is that by now it proves increasingly objectionable; so much so that all the unanswered questions it elicits tend to culminate in the query concerning possible alternatives.

These must necessarily flow forth from the basic concept of interaction, because this is a category in terms of process that can supplant the category known as objectification.

Reorientation: intersubjectivity and mutual relevance as key concepts

Pursuing this line of thought, one comes up, quite tentatively, with ideas in two directions. (1) Insofar as interaction involves agent, one arrives at the intersubjectivity concept that we have so frequently used already, as a valid indication for any condition of plural occurrence of sociocultural entities involving mutual relevance (of whatever kind) between them. Continuing in the same line, one ends up with an understanding of reality as composed of incidental clusters of mutually relevant instances of process, constituting plural sociocultural entities. This

[2] Georges Gusdorf, *Introduction aux sciences sociales* (Paris, Belles Lettres, 1960).

elegantly closes one circle of argument. (2) Insofar as interaction is more or less complex action, the possibility must be envisaged to ana- lytically distinguish between distinct aspects of an operational nature. Pursuing this line further one arrives at operationally distinct aspects of (instances of) reality each amenable to a particular discipline as the means to render it intelligible.

Disciplines as aspect-wise approaches to operationally conceived reality

In consequence, disciplines would turn out to be aspect-wise approaches, on the part of the mind, for specific purposes of interaction with reality. The virtual interrelatedness of the several approaches that the mind could develop would be a necessary, pre-established datum: in such a way that it should prove fully workable any time a relevance between given approaches for given purposes would be established. In case a particular approach in dealing with its particular aspect of reality would prove to relate more frequently to certain particularly defined entities, this should be fully acceptable. On the other hand, it could never con- stitute exclusivity as a matter of principle.

One of the major gains to be reaped from this kind of development, in addition to finding a solution for the integration problem, would be that one could dispense with all the strife involved hitherto in ever new specialisms fighting for a place under the sun against established interests of recognized disciplines and specialisms. No manner of dealing with reality could ever achieve more than an *ad hoc* status. Sometimes one obtains the impression that in science a development in this direction is already well under way. But such matters are hard to judge for a social scientist who, of course, may feel inclined to believe that neighbour's lawn is greener.

22

THEORY AND PRACTICE

In order to complete this prospect, something remains to be added to what was said before on the relationship between theory and practice. Within a framework of objectification, practice is traditionally conceived as the application of theory to "reality": a curious, somehow Platonic, theory-centric one-sidedness. It inevitably presupposes the relevance of general theory to the specific situation to which it is applied; but in the course of time this relevance as such, along with the connection between general and specific, have tended to appear increasingly problematic. We have been brought up in the devout belief that theory cannot overrule facts: but insofar as we try to behave, the application of theory may prove either a matter of brinkmanship or a most disconcerting experience. For lack of a clear moment of acute crisis, the "application urge" tends to linger on. In development situations this often means that for all practical purposes the colonial administrator's approach to current matters continues virtually unaltered under conditions of independence *cum* development assistance.

On the other hand, the tremendously increased role of research is an unmistakable indication that beneath the surface things have been changing for some time and continue to change even more. A state of affairs is beginning to appear in which theory is one element in the "steering" component of a given development situation, and research one element of its "feed-back" component. The relative importance of either element in regard to other elements contributing to steering and feed-back respectively is a rather hazy matter for the time being. This, however, cannot detract from their actual and potential significance.

The significance of the scholar's role; and "théorie engagée"

It is interesting to see where this places the scholar. In ever more effectively interrelating theory with research, he is likely to end up, in the framework of a development process, in a capacity that could closely resemble the innovative function as defined and discussed above. The natural consequence seems to be that even insofar as he would be bound to remain a theorist, his will be a *théorie engagée*.

Considered in an entirely practical perspective, this shift seems to be neatly represented by a beginning shift both in terminology, and in actual involvement of those who are supposed to know and stimulate within given development situations. There is a tendency to speak of international co-operation rather than of aid or assistance. This is largely a matter of yet another fashion in polite diplomatic terminology, but it cannot be entirely written off as such.

The involved expert

Furthermore, as against the expert, we witness the emergence of the person who comes to share in a development process, be he a Peace Corps volunteer going abroad or an Iranian Literacy Corps member submerging for a time in some out-of-the-way village. The expert usually knows his trade to perfection but has no real chance to know the context into which this knowledge is going to be injected. The Corps member is normally too young to be much of an expert in anything, but he has the preparation and the mental readiness to share the life of those whom his work is supposed to help. Of course, the pendulum could swing too far, but there is no doubt that sharing the conditions of life is an indispensable asset if it comes to pointing out possibilities or desirabilities. There is really nothing new in all this; it is just that in regard to development there has been a tendency to skip such all-too-normal considerations.

One of the main things about development is perhaps that we have to stop dramatizing it as something altogether extraordinary. As long as we go on considering it as such, we are in principle exonerated any time we bungle a job. It is by considering it as something perhaps novel but entirely within the order of the day, that we shall be more ready to envisage it, and deal with it, in a matter-of-fact manner, *sine ira et studio*.

23

EDUCATION FOR DEVELOPMENT

Certain practical consequences remain to be drawn in regard to education or training for development.

There are two main aspects to this matter. One is the problem of how to set up and maintain an educational system in a given development situation (if you like, developing country) that will adequately account for prevailing developmental needs: civic, cultural and economic. The other refers to educational assistance; and one may apply a further division of subject matter according to whether the assistance is given on the spot, in the development situation concerned, or elsewhere.

Within the present framework it is impossible to do justice to the subject in its full length and width. It seems therefore appropriate to select one aspect only, for more or less exemplary discussion. The following observations will thus be restricted to educational facilities made available in so-called developed countries for people from developing countries who are expected to be involved in development action, one way or another, upon their return home.[1] From the various levels at which such facilities are offered, we select only the higher ones, again

---

[1] Some may feel that this is putting the stress at the wrong end. It is more or less fashionable, right now, to speak of educational assistance in a manner suggesting, or taking for granted, that a necessary shift will increase the number of educational facilities "at home" for students in developing countries and accordingly lessen the need for "study abroad". The argument that will follow here in the text will be based on the following considerations. (1) There is no saying how fast or slow this shift will be: for the time being any increase in facilities at home will strengthen rather than lessen the need for study abroad. (2) The argument may be correct for "educational assistance" in the usual sense of the word: but, as will be implicitly argued, this sense is open to challenge. There is more to education for development than merely assistance by transferring some (usually rather narrowly defined) skills. (3) The internationalization in higher education and research, particularly referring to matters of change and development, is likely to, and indeed has a need to increase and to be made ever more effective.

for no other purpose than to achieve reasonable limitations to what could be discussed here.

Training abroad

A carry-over from the days when development was technological development is the idea that education or training for development, provided in developed countries to people from developing countries, is a matter of transferring skills. The skills concerned, in their turn, are tacitly or explicitly assumed (1) to be available where they are offered for transfer and (2) to be relevant where they are to be used by those to whom they will have been transferred. The idea of the transfer of skills does not usually seem to receive all the thorough critical inspection it deserves. Indeed it survives a considerable amount of changes in other respects, including change in definitions of development proper.

If questions have arisen in the connection, they have usually referred to the apparent complication caused by the cross-cultural nature of the transfer. It was felt that the student may not be ideally conditioned, "culturally", for proper absorption of what had to be instilled into his mind. Consequently, it was to be feared that he might fail to carry his new skills with him unimpaired, or alternatively that he might fail to put them to proper use upon his return.

Education for students from developing areas: three trends

However, upon closer consideration it appears that more or less hidden behind this kind of questions there are further, and perhaps even more important issues. In order to focus these properly, it is useful first to say a few more words on some divergent tendencies that have gradually become visible in higher education offered in developed countries to students from developing countries. There are at least three clearly distinguishable trends, plus a number of in-between variants.

One is to let students from developing countries participate as regular students in the programmes normally offered to nationals of the country concerned. The assumption then is clearly a variation upon the old theme of "what is good for General Motors is good for the U.S.A.": what is good for an American, a Frenchman, an Englishman to know is good for an Iranian, an Indonesian, a Tanzanian to learn. That this line of reasoning is a neat case of Western ethnocentrism does not seem to bother too many of the Westerners concerned; nor, remarkable fact, does it seem to affect the demand by non-Western students. Some maintain that this is so because a major concern to them is the status that a degree from a Western university confers: typical carry-over from colonial days with their principle of "concordant" education in colony and mother country.

The second trend is to offer special courses for people who will be active in development, independent of the regular offerings of universities in the developed country concerned, and if need be by institutions specially created for the purpose. Academic status may cause quite some problems in the connection, both for the agency concerned and for alumni. A countervailing advantage is the opportunity, in principle, to disregard customary Western pecularities in the teaching of the subject matter concerned and accordingly to allow for the specific requirements of development situations. Unfortunately, the main consequence is that this begs the question as to nature, scope and implications of these specific requirements.

The third trend is considerably less characterized by an effort to cater for the specific educational or training needs of students from developing countries. Even if it involves people from developing countries – sometimes in mixed roles as student and as informant – it is primarily the effort, of Western scholars, to understand development problems: whether purely academic or with further purposes such as training or counseling. A chance implication of such studies is that they may contribute to moulding the future shape of relationships between developed and underdeveloped, Western and non-Western parts of the world.

Prerequisites to educational offerings

The basic difficulty that is common to these three trends, although it will appear differently in each, is the relationship between knowns and unknowns. In this regard, problems like the hazards of cross-cultural transfer are mere symptoms of a more fundamental kind of problem. Phrased in a somewhat too demagogic manner, this problem is whether "we" have the knowledge that is adequate to the nature and complexity of the subject matter that we try to tackle. It does not take an alarmist or other kind of pessimist to recognize that the answer is in the negative.

Until Western scholarship, particularly in the social sciences, will manage to liberate itself effectively from its two main scourges, namely objectivism and ethnocentrism, the tools with which we tackle our problem are bound to be ill-fitting, and the consequences of using them nevertheless will be accordingly hazardous. It is not really long ago that some of us were upholding to non-Westerners, as the norm for political development, an ideal image of democracy that in the West itself attracts lip service at the very best.

The proper study of development

This being so, it is a matter of simple realism to recognize that in many regards the problem of development constitutes the vanguard battle of scholarship, particularly in the social sciences. Battle, moreover, that cannot be expected to yield any results but on the basis of open exchange, that is full scholarly co-operation, between Western and non-Western scholars. To achieve this could not be easy; but the easy alternative is not available.

It appears that in this light the first and third trend just listed should indeed not be separate. Progress in higher education and research is more likely to ensue from a consistent attempt to integrate the matter of development (which after all is world-wide and not the exclusive characteristic of "developing countries") into the normal curriculum, and to effectively internationalize the studies devoted to it.

Special training programmes: the important features

The consequence of this is that fundamentally there is no good reason for letting special agencies with special programmes cater for the special needs of students from developing countries and thus ultimately for the study of that special kind of problem known as development. Even so, development problems being as significant as they are for contemporary world relationships, there is wisdom in not carrying fundamental conclusions like these too far. More specifically, there is reason to ask whether it should be possible, in developed countries, to offer training to those nationals of developing countries who, in the relative peace of mind that a period of absence from home and from normal duties and involvements can offer, will try to acquire additional abilities to work toward development. More precisely, the question is what sort of training should then be offered.

It does not appear that the transfer of skills should be ruled out as one ingredient of such a programme. But it may not be the central consideration, nor would it have to be a matter of unmodified transfer. As regards the latter point: over and above acquiring skills that he may take home for application, the student will need to be sensitized to the necessity to check for the applicability of such skills under specific circumstances, and to be aware of alternative variants of application. What really matters here is that he should be the master, not the mere carrier or instrument of his skills. Whatever he will do at home is bound to have as its frame of reference not the Western context in which his skills were handed over to him (if ever he be made adequately aware of this context) but the range of development goals that determines conditions in his home town, country or whatever. He must be made to look out for that frame of reference and to account for it in his use of the skills he will have acquired abroad.

Over and above this – and here we reach the matter of central considerations – he should be offered an opportunity to build up for himself the particular orientation and bent of mind that should enable him to be effective as a development worker. What this means may first be expressed negatively: he should somehow be rendered less liable to be carried away by the general atmosphere, common to most developing countries, of politicization of anything and everything. More positively, over and above being taught particular skills, disciplines or bodies of theory, or even methods for work and research, he should be brought under conditions that will incite him to become an effective decision maker,[2] capable to distinguish between short-run and long-run considerations, between general interest and particular interest, between that which matters more in a given context and that which matters less. The easy way out is to indoctrinate him and to make him use the doctrine as a ready reckoner for any decision making he will have to do. This is too easy to be good: what it creates is slaves, not free people. The real challenge here is to let these abilities emerge without recourse to easy-but-false solutions: enabling the man to use his own considerate reading of conditions as the frame of reference for his decision-making and action.

Who qualifies for admission to training facilities?

Inevitably, all this involves motivation. Programmes with goals like these are useless to – and have no use for – students whose main goal in life is a few letters behind their names, for status purposes. Surely status counts, but it does not decide all.

If it is difficult to arrange for training in the manner here envisaged, this is so because of two factors. One is that a programme like this, academically as well as in terms of general orientation, is not easy to make; and good examples are lacking. The other is that not everybody could be a good participant, and, selection procedures being what they

[2] This point has recently been argued in a challenging way by Y. Dror in *Civilisations*, Vol. XVII, No. 112 (Bruxelles, 1967), pp. 72-79.

are anyway, it should be extremely hard to select the right candidates. There are difficulties especially in two respects.

First, some candidates will usually turn up who prove to have grave difficulty in trying to envisage themselves, even for purely experimental purposes, as devoid of the sheltered existence of their own circles: this as a means to achieve a direct and all-out confrontation with live development problems, – whether of the city or – even more remote prospect – of the countryside. It is unpleasant but perhaps inevitable to note that the probability of such candidates turning up has increased rather than decreased with the increase, over the years, of governmental interference in selection procedures: both in the "giving" and in the "receiving" countries. Perhaps inevitably, the government-sponsored candidate will have a natural commitment to a specific understanding of a given state of affairs. In some cases, this may mean that development features in a very specific meaning, as a given government policy; in other cases it may even appear as a risk rather than as a goal worth striving for. In the free pursuit of scholarly insight, the government-sponsored candidate is inevitably under some constraints, if not formal at least moral.

On the other hand, some candidates turn up, including government-sponsored ones, who sound all-out rebellious and inordinately critical of prevailing conditions, in their own countries and perhaps in most of the world. Many of them will be quite alike the other kind in that they are prone to indulge in merely verbal criticisms, speculative theorizing and slogan-like panaceas, whilst avoiding to get their hands dirty.

As against all this, it appears beyond doubt that the real hope for the future lies with candidates to whom the freedom and security of academe is a jumping board from which they will not fail to take the plunge in due course of time.

This now leads to the question where to look for such candidates. Who indeed, are the ones who will be effective development workers?

PART VI

DEVELOPMENT:
A CHALLENGE TO WHOM?

DEVELOPMENT: WHOSE CONCERN?

Final question: if development constitutes a challenge, as is so often and so easily said, who gets challenged? There are in this connection two kinds of questions. They are entirely crucial to the practice of development. Besides, they have the virtue that they bring into focus a number of the preceding considerations. Thus, the attempt to answer them can at the same time serve as a partial summing-up.

The one question elaborates the original query concerning "who?". It is about which category or categories of people in a given development situation will assume something like a protagonist's role; or, to use a term already discussed, who will fulfil the function of the agent of development.

The other question refers to the manner in which they will do so. More specifically, it refers to the link that they envisage between development as process and development as action.

Three candidates for the role of development agent

There are at least three answers to the former question. It is perhaps symptomatic for development conditions that they are not merely different but in fact competitive. Their differences ensue from differences in underlying interpretation in regard to control over development (and thus, basically, in regard to control over sociocultural process as such). Partly this is an empirical matter: who has control; for another part it is normative: who should control.

First now, a brief listing of the three categories that tend to feature as candidates for the role of development agent. In listing them, one must set out from the realization that the prelude to the emergence of a development situation, whether outright decolonization or some parallel process, eliminates both the bearers of foreign rule and the bearers of the nationalist struggle against such rule. With the decolonization process, also its main actors disappear from the scene. By the same token, whatever remnants of a traditional elite may have weathered, and to an extent perhaps even survived, colonial days, will hardly be in a position to qualify for the role now under consideration.

The candidates one does find are the following,

(1) a category or categories of people somehow identified with development as promoted by aid offered by developed to underdeveloped countries;

(2) a category or categories of people somehow identified with development as the assertion of selfhood of the sociocultural entity concerned: usually the direct successors to the nationalists of the struggle for independence;

(3) a category or categories of people somehow identified with the urgent and immediate need for drastic betterment of conditions.

The first and second categories are two variants of the type "those who have control"; the third represents the type "those who would control".

There is no shortage of epithets that one could use for further description and elucidation of these three categories.

1. *Westernizers*

Amongst the first category, one would find the westernizers and assimilationists (not to say acculturationists) of late colonialism and their heirs, who continue to believe that the formula of universal cultural assimilation is the correct answer to the needs of today's one world. As argued above, they may be mistaken. Even so, there is no denying that in their midst one does not merely find the die-hard culture imperialists, but well-intended, almost naive minds as well. It is this category that will produce the staunch adherents to a "free world" allegiance, siding with the Western powers in the cold war. People of this bent of mind, whether Europeans and North Americans or so-called non-Westerners, are probably more influential in any kind of development aid activities than people with a different outlook. This category is evolutionary in orientation, not entirely without a Western-centric bias.

2. *Neo-nationalists*

Amongst the second category one must rate in the first place the power wielding group(s) in many, if not most, developing countries. Neo-nationalists out of necessity equally much as out of conviction, they identify with the maintenance and promotion of their own, often relatively recently created, nation-states. Inevitably preoccupied to a considerable extent by precarious balancing, both nationally and internationally, between countless, ever shifting and often mutually contrary forces, they will typically tend to adopt a neutralist stand in regard to world-wide matters like the cold war. By the same token, their activities on the national plane may indicate a preference for short-run expeditiousness over long-run constructivism. Potential monopolists of development, they are bound to be tempted to envisage development as the main justification for the control they exert and simultaneously as the major means to maintain and promote this control. This category is neither necessarily evolutionary nor necessarily revolutionary in outlook, inasmuch as from its viewpoint any work for the future, such as development work, must needs have the present *status quo* as its decisive frame of reference.

3. *Subversives*

The third category is a somewhat more complex proposition. Basically it consists of the indigent, the suffering masses, the underdogs of any society. But factually it is made visible and rendered effective by those, hardly ever numerous, who decide to identify with them, to speak on their behalf, and more important, to instill into them an awareness of their condition, a self-view, and ensuing therefrom, a potential capability to act.[1]

To these two elements must be added a third that somehow joins them together: the model to which, in acquiring a self-awareness and in assuming goals for action, they will conform. This model has for a considerable time been promulgated, and generally believed in, as something singular and basically simple. It was the model of Marxism, of revolutionary action by the exploited groups of a given society. Ever since Stalin ventured into designing a strategy for associating the oppressed colonial masses with the cause of the communist revolution,[2] it has become increasingly clear that the formula is not as simple and as effective as it may have seemed at first.

[1] Comp. R. Debray, *Révolution dans la révolution* (Paris, Le Nouvel Observateur, 1967). For a shattering but not quite unjustified verdict on Debray and his admirers comp. Leopold de Buch, "Wissenschäftler aller Länder, vereinigt Euch!", *Het Hollands Maandblad* (Feb. 1968), pp. 14-18. Comp. also Pike's argument that the Viet Cong stress organization of the people prior to action prior to indoctrination: D. Pike, *Viet Cong, The Organization and Techniques of the National Liberation Front of South Viet Nam* (Cambridge, Mass., M.I.T., 1966).
[2] J. Staline, *Le Marxisme et la question nationale et coloniale* (Paris, Ed. Sociales, 1949).

Gradually, the point has been reached where a fundamentally Western, Marxist-Leninist variant has become distinct from a newly emerging non-Western, post-Marxian variant.[3] In maximizing the organization, for offensive purposes, of any underdog mass and in categorically identifying any category of established wielders of power as exploitative,[4] this latter variant is somehow more sophisticated than the former. Unfortunately, this may mean that it is also more tempted to be nihilistic in its totalitarianism. At the same time its capability for subversion is virtually unlimited.

This category has considerable appeal, both to people inside a particular development situation and to onlookers from outside. It is therefore appropriate to devote a few more words to the base of this appeal. They set out from a given fact: the visible differences between those in control and "the masses". They offer two readings of it simultaneously, not bothering to rhyme one with the other. According to the one, this is neo-colonialism: the colonial structure revived [5] after the successful colonial revolution, by a ruthless category of new men, nationals of the newly independent state, who do not hesitate to follow in the footsteps of the earlier foreign colonizers and who to this purpose will connive with their former masters if the opportunity arises. According to the other explanation, this is exploitation, by a privileged class, of an underdog class, a proletariat. No doubt, the proletariat remains to be defined, and this is where not all communists agree.

On the basis of these two explanations, they attempt to identify the forces of betterment-through-revolution. In so doing they run into the already mentioned dilemma between doctrinaire explanations of reality (it seems that this is one of the meanings of that ominous word, Stalinism) and realism. Where realism prevails, there is a manifest inclination to go for the poor rural masses on the one hand and a category sometimes called the unattached,[6] often consisting of students and the like, on

---

[3] L. Bianco, *Les origines de la révolution chinoise, 1915-1949* (Paris, NRF: Idées, 1967), takes great care to point out the distinctive novel elements; see esp. pp. 127-132, 137 jo. 184, 307, 348 f.

[4] Considered in this perspective the shift from urban industrial proletariat to suffering peasants is more than an incidental change in choice of underdog category: it affects the very time-and-place conditioned character of a number of considerations basic to Marxism.

[5] At least one out of the numerous books that have appeared on the occasion of the recent celebration of the communist revolution in Russia explains the creation of the U.S.S.R. along precisely these lines: Eugene Lyons, *Workers' Paradise Lost* (New York, Funk & Wagnalls, 1967; paperback edition, New York, Twin Circle Paperback Library, 1967).

[6] Mary Morse, *The Unattached* (Harmondsworth, Penguin, 1965).

the other hand. Particularly where the appeal succeeds in bringing the two together in some construct suggesting or actually promoting a community of interest and of ensuing zeal, a proposition results that will indeed appear attractive. More so since one is led to believe that here finally is one serious attempt to identify and mobilize (organize and motivate) the real forces of development.

Upon further consideration, unfortunately not much of this hopeful picture remains. These forces are geared to subversion, and theoretically to revolution. Unfortunately, where Western Marxism and non-Western neo-Marxism are in full accord is that neither has a workable prescription for the day after the successful revolution.

Be this as it may, the third category here under review is explicitly and emphatically revolutionary, with a bias towards a doctrine that is labeled Marxism and that leaves a basic uncertainty of orientation: whether towards Moscou or Peking or, neo-neutralist fashion,[7] towards neither.

The three categories are necessarily competitive

Each of the three categories listed is, on top of all the characteristics mentioned, characterized by a calling to act toward development. Inasmuch as many if not most development situations show a presence of the three simultaneously, their already signalled competitive relationships deserve some further scrutiny. To this purpose, the second consideration referred to above must enter into the picture as well: the manner in which each category envisages its function as the development agent.

In this respect, one anticipates the clearest opposition in appreciations between the first and the third category, with the second wavering uneasily in between. In regard to the first the adjective evolutionist has already been used, and in regard to the third we have spoken of revolutionary.

The three categories and their choices of development goals

There is more to this than the mere opposition of two basic philosophies concerning social process. Indeed, one runs here into the reflection of a basic and inevitable contradiction inherent in development goals and by implication also in development policies. It is particularly manifest in the case of former colonies that have achieved independence; but it

[7] Indeed, the orientation of Cuba, North Korea and perhaps also North Vietnam could be appropriately called neo-neutralist.

features virtually without exception in all development situations. On the one hand development aims at the realization of a state of affairs that will in no way appear as less satisfactory than what "the West" has achieved. On the other hand, development aims quite explicitly at the affirmation and fostering of specific non-Western characteristics proper to a particular society, whereby this society will maintain, in the world context of today, a status of equality with others. This contradiction is often obscured because in either case the West features as some sort of norm: in the one case for purposes of imitation, in the other for emulation. The importance of development aid is a further factor that will hide the contradiction from sight, particularly on the part of Western observers.

Now consider this. Under the circumstances, the discussion concerning development goals tends to be determined mainly by the definition from which one will – often tacitly – set out. At this point, it is necessary to return to a line of argument already developed above.

On the one hand – and this is in a way the older perception – one may conceive of development primarily as technological development, as was customary immediately after World War II. If so, then one arrives necessarily at technological goals for development. A good example that even now has not lost its importance is industrialization; remember also Gandhi's opposition to industrialization. Similarly, one may conceive of development primarily as the improvement of material conditions of life. Then, one arrives in equally self-evident manner at goals that are more or less exclusively economic, such as increase of annual *per capita* income, improvement of economic infrastructure and the like. This relatively simplistic approach is broadly speaking the vision of the first category.

On the other hand, there exists a different view; in a way this is also the later one. Gradually more and more shifts have occurred in the definitions of development. Indeed the concept shows a tendency towards broadening all the time. Consequently the query concerning development goals leads less and less to simple and self-evident responses. The consequence that is drawn by certain people is to envisage development as a comprehensive phenomenon. Not stopping there, however, some also foreshorten its time perspective into one moment or quite brief period of crucial action, of inevitably revolutionary nature. This now is briefly the standpoint of the third category. It is perhaps necessary to clarify that this standpoint does not in every respect represent the more recent developments in the development concept. Insofar as it appreciates and underscores its comprehensiveness, it is indeed up-to-date. Insofar as it condenses the inherent time sequence into one critical moment it represents a curious and willful relapse into a historicistic, if not a-historical, doctrine that is undoubtedly revolutionary but that, more important, is in the same way timeless and placeless as platonism, utopianism and virtually any kind of chiliastic expectation: it short-circuits logical with sociocultural categories.

Doctrine, whether conscious or unconscious, enters into the picture on either side in yet another manner. This time it refers to the norm or model to which development is somehow assumed to have to conform.

In the former case it is, in the last resort, a variant of Western ethnocentrism, even if perhaps represented by non-Westerners. In the latter case it is a variant of the scheme of prescriptive historicism developed by Marx. All this could be neither important nor particularly harmful if it were as simple and as manifest as it appears in the preceding sentences.

The reason why such simplicity and clarity are lacking lies in the stand that people belonging to any of our three categories are bound to take in regard to the relationship between development as action and development as process.

The critical step: from conspectus of development goals to plan

Let it be assumed that in a given development situation someone would have succeeded in identifying, along the lines elaborated above, a full set of development goals, each with a rating of its relative significance, and all of them together understood in their actual mutual relationships. Let it further be assumed that people belonging to any one of the three categories discussed above will attempt to produce a development plan and subsequently to implement development policies according to this plan. Then, there are bound to occur differences between the set of identified development goals on the one hand, and development plan plus policy on the other. These differences are necessitated by the need to make plan and policy optimally effective: the need, in other words, for them to be adopted by public opinion and to be acted upon with a reasonable measure of concerted action. The development goals constituting the plan are bound to represent a simplified and eclectic presentation of actually identifiable development goals in the context concerned. Moreover, it is usually assumed, although seldom argued,[8]

[8] Albert O. Hirschman and Charles E. Lindblom, "Economic Development, Research and Development, Policy Making: Some Converging Views", *Behav-*

that the consistency in a development plan will have to be considerably greater than the consistency in the development situation concerned. When speaking of goal-setting one tends to imply a complex of choices resulting in an effort to steer purposely in a particular direction. Indeed, the difference between the goals inherent in a development situation and the goals constituting a development plan follows from a complex of choices and further arbitrary acts committed by those constituting the category of people actually or potentially fulfilling the function of the development agent.

The crucial question here is how they will arrive at decisions of arbitration, and using which norm or yardstick. It is precisely at this point that westernizing bias and Marxist doctrine enter into the picture: not as lowly temptations but on the contrary as necessary aids at a crucial moment of decision making. It is in a way the fundamental weakness of the second category, the neo-nationalists, that in matters like these they are bound to be neutralist: that is, for all practical purposes, normless; and we know how closely normlessness and alienation are related. On the other hand, this is a weakness that yet may yield strength, in the form of flexibility and versatility, and also in the ability to steer clear of some of the tangles just mentioned.

We have thus far mainly spoken about two of the three categories. In returning now to the matter of their mutually competitive relationships, there will be an opportunity to pay some more attention to the second on the list, which is in many respects in a middle position.

The competition between the three categories

Between the first and the third category there are fundamental differences in outlook on various counts, as listed. The Cold War formula is added to all this as an easy and simple summing-up and rationalization: it freezes the competition into an effective deadlock. The consequence is, according to some, a permanent stalemate, euphemistically styled containment; and according to others an all-out struggle involving survival. It may sound academic, but it is nevertheless important to note that the introduction of the Cold War formula at this point is a pernicious falsification. It presents in oversimplified black-and-white form a contrast that is in fact highly complex and far from clear: less so since on either side a considerable number of considerations are in-

---

ioral Science (Ann Arbor, Mich., Apr. 1962), pp. 211-222; also as Doc. P-1982, The Rand Corporation (Santa Monica, Calif.); French transl. *Bulletin SEDEIS* 896 suppl. (Paris, 20 Sep. 1964), mimeo.

volved that have not been thought out in anything like an adequate or definitive fashion, and also a number of issues that have wittingly or unwittingly been left largely unresolved. Take the idea of westernization: it inevitably assumes the West to be an identifiable entity and a constant, but neither assumption is correct. Exactly the same sort of doubts are called for in regard to Marxist doctrine.

The competition between our first and third categories reflects in the relationships of each to the second. Interestingly there is a significant ambiguity in either case; but this is where the similarity ends.

The westernizers will be inclined to look upon the neo-nationalists with a mixture of suspicion and paternalism. On the whole, however, they will be inclined to act on the assumption that between them there exists a natural identity of goals and orientations, a natural alliance. The suspicion derives from the circumstance that the westernizers fail to see the good sense in the stress on independent selfhood that to the neo-nationalists is a vital consideration. Even so, a taste for gradualism and meliorism, a type of constructiveness that tends to avoid the losses ensuing from strife and clashes, and furthermore the realization that confusion is inherent in development and also the urge to build out of confusion rather than to confound it more; – all these appear to be common bonds.

On the other hand, the subversives have no use whatsoever for the neo-nationalists: except one, and that is a vital one, namely to use them as scapegoats. Here again the antagonism is not strong enough to eliminate the underlying basic ambivalence. As often as not the monster of revolution is held caged and all that is kept going is subversion. At the same time the old recipe to prepare for revolution through alliance with the nationalists is carried over, unjustifiedly no doubt, to the relationship between contemporary subversives and neo-nationalists. The revolution is crucial, it is impending, but it is not immediately effective. In the interval those in power are prodded along to commit ever more errors, to become ever more corrupt, to elicit ever more opposition and to cause ever more unrest and dissatisfaction. All these are, quite optimistically, assumed to play into the cause of the revolution: revolution that can be unleashed at any time deemed appropriate by the masterminds of the party. In their turn, the neo-nationalists tend to be outright antagonistic to the subversives, to the point of turning a deaf ear even to justified blames thrown upon them, – for two reasons, both of them valid. First, they are not ready to let themselves be ousted from control over society. Secondly and perhaps more important, they know that a successful revolution, besides being sure to bring another group to power, offers no guarantee whatsoever for instant bliss.

The complex tripartite stalemate that appears to ensue is further aggravated by the way in which the champions of the cold war tend to throw in their weight.

Aggravating effect of "outside" forces

On the one hand, the U.S.S.R. and the Chinese People's Republic, in mutual competion, will not merely support (morally and at times materially) the subversives, but they will at the same time maintain relationships with the neo-nationalist category. These will not merely reflect in their turn the ambivalence between subversives and neo-nationalists just described: they will additionally reflect ambiguities ensuing from the cold war. Thus the U.S.S.R. may outbid the U.S.A. in offering the U.A.R. aid for the construction of the High Dam: at a time when the Egyptian communists and the Nasser regime are locked in a deadly embrace.

On the other hand, the so-called Western powers, the U.S.A. in the forefront and the others following in their customary, most unconcerted fashion, tend to take the westernizers for granted as some sort of extension of themselves. This leads occasionally to surprises and even to usually unexpected rebuffs. Their attitude towards the neo-nationalists is as a rule benevolent. This is not merely a matter of desiring to avoid at any cost that they would appear subversive. Nor is it merely a matter of wishing to avoid adding to existing confusion and existing waste of effort. To an considerable extent it is based on a deeply rooted respect for legitimacy and for what is considered to be international fair play, according to inherited rules of diplomacy and the like.

Inevitably there are also complicating factors. For example, practically everywhere business is not merely ultra-nationalist and at times protectionist, but also expansive and what is nowadays called aggressive: up to the point where many may feel justified in calling it neo-colonist or neo-imperialist. Besides, it has effective ways of influencing its national policy. In view of the deep dissatisfactions that tend to manifest themselves at occasions like the New Delhi Conference of U.N.C.T.A.D., it is curious that the role of business in contemporary international relations is thoroughly studied from the economic point of view but is at the same time virtually neglected so far as its social and political implications are concerned: whether "at home" or, more particularly, "abroad". If more were clear in this regard there might perhaps be less occasion to decry business as the villain in the piece.

Be this as it may, the relationship between Western powers and neo-nationalists is not without its inherent ambivalences. The latter are bound to hold back on the relationship if only to safeguard their independent identity, and also because they are not clear about the limits to which they can safely and freely associate with the Western powers. These in their turn tend to cherish the image of a natural alliance, but inasmuch as this relationship seems more or less automatically to place them in a never ending donor position, there are bound to be echoes from earlier colonial days. The relationship threatens to be marred by inequalities at a moment when those concerned are oversensitive about equality.

The inevitable consequence, in Cold War terms, is that the Western powers blame the communist powers for promoting subversion for no other purpose than to grab power and whilst avoiding to offer real help towards the solution of urgent development problems elsewhere. Conversely, the communist block blame the "free world" block for upholding corrupt and incompetent power cliques that do not deserve to see the light of the next morning. There is a measure of truth in either accusation; but both risk proving false precisely insofar as they neglect to account for the limits within which this truth obtains.

What can lead to competition may also engender latitude for movement

Hitherto we have seen how in every development situation there is a twice complicated answer to the question, to whom development constitutes a challenge. There are at least three categories of potential agents of development. In the international perspective behind them one distinguishes the major forces operative in today's world-wide context. Development is as much a national as an international issue, and in both regards it is subject to a good deal of confusion.

This confusion appears, on the one hand, as competition, with ensuing mutual positions that seem to be ever hardening. The often discussed phenomenon of radicalization comes to mind in the connection. On the other hand, the same confusion appears as lack of clarity or vagueness: and we shall have to say more about this aspect in a while.

The fourth category not to be overlooked

Prior thereto, another consideration enters into the argument. It refers to those to whom development does not immediately appear to constitute a challenge: the common man, those who somehow do not qualify for inclusion in one of the three categories discussed above. Whatever one may have to say about these categories, they have in common that in the last resort they are elitist: the common bond between the members of each is that they play or intend to play an elitist role. It is quite curious that in this regard development shows nothing but the return, under a new guise, of the ages-old pattern.

Here lies the crucial problem and the potential tragedy of development: even those who are aware that a new game must be played, cannot avoid relapsing into old rules when attempting to play it. The crux of the matter lies in the question whether the category or categories functioning, or aspiring to function, as development agents will and can envisage their function in such a way that its elitist trait will remain instrumental and not become purposive. No doubt, there is no shortage of lip service being paid to this consideration. Yet there is a most disconcerting shortage of effective action in accordance with such recognitions. Curiously, it is precisely the competition between the candidates for the role of development agent that will usually be quoted as the excuse.

Even so, what really matters in development is that its challenge should ever more be conceived as in no way restrictive. It must be seen as applying not merely to one particular category, in the development agent's role, but on the contrary as applying to everybody who exists in the given development situation. The crucial feature of development is increasing participation.

No doubt, to any given person's effective participation in a particular matter there are bound to occur more or less natural limitations. But the danger in development situations is that a person may never have an opportunity to participate up to those natural limits, because some division of roles in regard to development, introduced by a development agent or otherwise, would impose other, arbitrary limits. In the long run such limits are likely to thwart development rather than to promote it. In this regard, the three categories discerned are equally subject to dangerous temptations.

Rigid positions or claims and fixed formulas obstruct development

Returning now to the vagueness aspect of the confusion inherent in (under)development. If there is hope, it lies here.

Recall that development is in the last resort sociocultural process as such (that is, as argued above, sociocultural reality envisaged in the contemporary manner), with, as a particular feature, an emergent phenomenon that we have called above, *ad hoc* convergence. It is precisely the *ad hoc*, incidental, and basically fluid nature of the convergence that matters now. The reason is that it makes abundantly clear one crucial consideration that is as a rule overlooked and that is indeed bound to vanish from sight any time groups compete for the privilege of being *the* agent of development. Development goals, whether in the form of a set of goals carefully identified in a given development situation or in the simplified and streamlined form of a development plan *cum* policy, are necessarily *ad hoc*. No presentation of either can be assumed to be more than an attempt to catch a fleeting moment. The continued use of such a presentation depends very much on the flexibility with which it will be continuously adapted according to feed-back and new information received, and thus in the last resort on the degree to which those identified with plans etc. are open to never-ending shifts in reality.

Consequently, any rigid positions and any permanently staked claims (or putting the same more harshly, any monopolies of development) are fundamentally at odds with the essentials of a development situation. Nobody owns the recipe for development.

As mentioned, planners show an awareness of these fundamental realizations in attempting to produce ever more sophisticated, that is, ever more flexible plans. On the other hand, governments in their development policies sometimes give the impression of trying to maintain a haughty and potentially dangerous aloofness in regard to these basic considerations. There is a trend afoot to centralize and governmentalize any matters pertaining to development and specifically to development aid, which upon closer consideration seems unrealistic. For example the tendency, already mentioned, to channel scholarships and intellectual exchanges between developed and underdeveloped countries through government agencies, properly argued as it may seem with respect to dangers like the brain drain and subversion, is not merely at odds with academic freedom: it runs indeed counter against the desirability to let a broad range of varying ideas on development achieve maturity in order that each may offer a positive contribution.

Carrying this line of thought to its ultimate consequence, one ends up in what seems to be a dilemma. On the one hand, one must recognize that a wide variety of development impulses is a real and perhaps useful phenomenon. On the other hand, one recognizes the need, often exaggerated, for some consistency in order that plural development impulses may prove conducive in a particular, clear direction: and perhaps consistency is less important than selective stress and controlled strife. Whereas the former consideration evokes the classical idea of the market, the latter evokes leadership, a concept with rather mixed associations. What seems to matter is how to achieve a vision, and an ensuing pattern of action, according to which these two will not simply and fatally be one another's opposites, but on the contrary will constitute a complementarity, in the sense that the one will never achieve an impact such as to annihilate the other.

In practice, this amounts to a plea for a consistent effort at flexibility, both in development policies and in policies regarding development aid. Such flexibility would under no circumstances accord or recognize monopolies of development. Nor would it under any circumstances assume that what seemed appropriate yesterday will necessarily be the correct answer to the problems of tomorrow. Surely, these demands are not easy to meet. But who said that development is an easy matter?

Above all, development is a lesson for Promethean man. It teaches at once the limitations and the crucial importance of the human agent, whether person or group, in the framework of sociocultural process.

The challenge of development concerns us

A final word now on the three categories discussed above. It is worth noting that the degree of exclusivism, which partly relates to the elitist tendency already referred to, is not the same in each case. The westernizers are in principle non-exclusivist, the neo-nationalists are strongly tempted to be exclusivist, and the subversives are strongly inclined to avoid any conditions where they would have to choose. "Communism in one country" is, after all, a very old sore, and one that hurts ever more. The point in raising the matter here is that it offers an opportunity to repeat that fundamentally speaking, the distinction, in today's world, between autochthonous and foreign forces making for development in a given situation is false. It is a relapse into obsolete categories. In this perspective, it makes profound sense to answer the question who is challenged by development with the simple word "we". Now who exactly is this "we", if not a hollow rhetorical device or, worse still, Western ethnocentrism that, having been ceremoniously kicked out by the front door, is sneaking back in from behind? Answer in to-morrow's terms: "we" are the world citizens who have somehow to make ours a full human life in this world of close living. Answer in today's terms: "we" are those who care about what will happen to-morrow in our own society, therefore in the world as a whole, therefore in other people's societies. We may be at work in our own society, or for that matter in theirs. In theirs, we are aliens today, but the difference that this can make will be less tomorrow than it is today.

SUBJECT INDEX

AUTHORS' INDEX

STUDIES IN THE SOCIAL SCIENCES

edited by

C. A. O. van Nieuwenhuijze

1. C. A. O. van Nieuwenhuijze: *The Nation and the Ideal City: Three Studies in Social Identity.* 1966. 148 pp., 14 figs.
   f 21,50/$6.15

2. Jelle C. Riemersma: *Religious Factors in Early Dutch Capitalism 1550-1650.* 1967. 98 pp. *f* 14,—/$4.00

3. C. A. O. van Nieuwenhuijze: *Intelligible Fields in the Social Sciences.* 1967. 285 pp. *f* 36,—/$10.30

MOUTON · PUBLISHERS · THE HAGUE